SIX CHAPTERS FROM MY LIFE "DOWNUNDER"

Six Chapters
From My Life "Downunder"

Yang Jiang

Translated by Howard Goldblatt
With a Preface by Jonathan Spence

University of Washington Press
Seattle & London

The Chinese University Press
Hong Kong

A *Renditions Book* of the Research Center for Translation,
The Chinese University of Hong Kong
General editors: Stephen C. Soong and George Kao

Library of Congress Cataloging-in-Publication Data

Yang, Chiang.
  Six chapters from my life "downunder".

  Translation of: Kan hsiao liu chi.
  1. Yang, Chiang. 2. Authors, Chinese—20th century—
Biography. I. Title.
PL2922.C49Z46813   1984   895.1'35   84-2228
ISBN 0-295-96146-5 cl.
ISBN 0-295-96081-7 pbk.

84 85 86 87 88   5 4 3 2 1

Contents

Preface

Shen Fu's haunting *Six Chapters from a Floating Life* were written close to two centuries ago, and it is fascinating to see them reinvoked in Yang Jiang's *Six Chapters from My Life "Downunder."* The contexts of the two works could not seem more different, for Ms. Yang depicts the world of Chinese Communist correctional institutions in the late 1960s and early 1970s, whereas Shen wrote of the faded world of lower Confucian literati as the Qing dynasty slid past its prime at the end of the eighteenth century; yet Yang Jiang has recaptured Shen's moods with uncanny skill: in her work one finds a similar gentle melancholy concerning the individual's helplessness in the face of a tyrannical society, along with a similar celebration of the tiny victories that are made possible by aesthetic sensitivity or by the strength of personal love. Neither book claims to be an accurate portrayal of the "real" world in all its dimensions, but each is content to be—unabashedly—an intellectual's appraisal of how to withstand the harshness that surrounds us all. Yang Jiang complains less than Shen Fu, though she doubtless suffered more; and she has a wry sense of humor lacking in Shen. Furthermore, her most piercing passages transcend anything one can find in Shen, for she had a sharper schooling and has a sharper tongue.

Yang Jiang's statement that learning to accept the mud of China was, for her, "almost like having a loved one with a contagious disease" is the cruel yet exquisite stylistic foil for her reflection that "the waste produced in the cadre school was the best around." There can be few paired passages in Chinese literature that summarize the relations between the intellectuals, the peasantry and the forces of the state with such economy. Howard Goldblatt's translation is up to all these nuances, and brings us Yang Jiang's voice with integrity and tact. Through his translation Yang's *Six Chapters* become an unlikely but unbudgeable part of Western understanding of the Great Proletarian Cultural Revolution.

Jonathan Spence

About the Author

YANG JIANG 楊絳 (pen name of Yang Jikang 楊季康) was born in 1911. In the early 1930s, she was educated at Soochow University 東吳大學, Soochow, and Tsinghua University 清華大學, Peking, where she met and married the scholar-writer, Qian Zhongshu 錢鍾書. In 1935 they went abroad to study at Oxford University, where Qian earned his B. Litt. degree, and subsequently spent a year at Paris, where Yang furthered her major interest in Romance Literature and Languages. They went back to China after the outbreak of the Sino-Japanese war. Although she contributed essays and short stories to a number of established journals in the 30s and 40s, she is by nature a modest and retiring person.

It was not until 1942, after they settled down in the French concession of Shanghai, that she was urged to try her hand at writing plays. Her first comedy *Chenxin ruyi* 稱心如意 (*As You Desire*) was an instant success, and was followed by another triumph: *Nongzhen chengjia* 弄眞成假 (*The Cheat*). Both plays won critical acclaim. Her third play *Youxi renjian* 遊戲人間 (*Sport with the World*) was a farce but could also be considered serious drama. This might have influenced the direction of her final attempt, *Fengxu* 風絮 (*Windswept Blossoms*), which developed in tragic terms the vision of her earlier comedies. The play was translated by Edward Gunn and published in part in *Renditions* No.14 (Autumn 1980), and has now been included in *Twentieth Century Chinese Drama: An Anthology*, edited by Edward Gunn and published by Indiana University Press, 1983.

After 1949, Yang and Qian went back to Tsinghua University and taught English Literature there. Both joined the Institute of Literature of the Academy of Sciences after the university became an institute of technology. Yang served as a fellow of the Institute of Literature in 1953, then fellow of the Institute of Foreign Literature in 1964. Her translation of Le Sage's (1668-1747) *Gil Blas* from French was published in 1976. During the anti-rightist movement and the Cultural Revolution, Yang and Qian continued to do their research and translation in silence and as allowed by the circumstances. They were finally transferred to a cadre school in Henan for a period of two years in 1969. With the fall of the Gang of Four, they were rehabilitated as their institutes were reorganized under the Academy of Social Sciences, separated from the Academy of Sciences. Not only did they continue to write and publish, but some of their works became best sellers and some of their pre-1949 writings were reprinted. Her recent publications include:—

> *Translations: Xiao Laizi* 小癩子 *La Vida de Lazarillo de Tormes* from Spanish, 1978
> *Tang Jikede* 堂吉訶德 *Don Quijote* by Cervantes from Spanish, 1978, 2nd impression 1979

Works: *Ganxiao liuji* 幹校六記 (*Six Chapters from My Life "Downunder"*) 1981, translated by Howard Goldblatt, first published in *Renditions* No. 16, (Autumn, 1981)

Chunni ji 春泥集 (*Spring Soil*), six critical essays on European and Chinese narrative art, 1982

Xiju liangzhong 喜劇兩種 (*Two Comedies*), a reissue of *As You Desire* and *The Cheat*, 1983

About Qian Zhongshu

READERS OF THIS BOOK cannot fail to be drawn to the personality of Qian Zhongshu (Ch'ien Chung-shu 錢鍾書). This is not just because he happens to be the author's husband and one of the most illustrious figures in the academic and literary scene in China today, but because he too underwent the life "downunder."

For more details of Qian's life and career, readers are referred to the English translation of his *Fortress Besieged* by Jeanne Kelly and Nathan K. Mao (Indiana University Press, 1980), and to *Unwelcome Muse* by Edward Gunn (Columbia University Press, 1980). Qian and Yang complement each other perfectly. While Yang's major critical interest in literature has been fiction, she has, either deliberately or subconsciously, eschewed writing short stories and novels, the field in which Qian gained his reputation as a creative writer, and has written drama instead. Whereas her critical essays have dealt with *Don Quijote*, *Vanity Fair*, *The Dream of the Red Chamber*, Henry Fielding and Li Yü, Qian's critical writings have concentrated on literature in general and poetry in particular. This tacitly understood division of labor discloses a genuine literary partnership.

Among his recent publications, mention should be made of the following: his novel *Wei cheng* (*Fortress Besieged*), originally published in 1947, reissued by the People's Literature Press in 1980, when it became a best seller; the *Addenda* published in 1981 to his 4-volume monumental *opus*: *Guanzhui pian* 管錐篇, 1978, and the revision of his *Tanyi lu* 談藝錄 (*On the Art of Poetry*), originally published in 1948, due to be reissued soon. *Tanyi lu* devotes itself to the study of classical Chinese poetry and "Poetry Talks" from the Tang to Qing dynasties. It will link up with *Guanzhui pian*, which discusses Chinese classical literature from *The Book of Changes* and *The Book of Songs* to the complete pre-Tang prose. Together these two works will constitute a grand tour of Chinese literature over a period of more than three thousand years, a feat unprecedented in the annals of Chinese scholarship.

SIX CHAPTERS FROM MY LIFE "DOWNUNDER"

Foreword

After finishing her *Six Chapters from My Life "Down-under,"*[1] Yang Jiang asked me to look over the manuscript. I felt that she should have written one more chapter, which we can, for the moment, call "A Sense of Shame: Participating in Political Campaigns."

One of the important missions of the Studies Division cadre school was to carry on a political campaign, specifically to ferret out "May Sixteenth elements."[2] Thus the more than two years we lived at the cadre school were spent in an atmosphere of criticism and struggle. The rhythm of this political campaign tightened and relaxed in accordance with other needs such as farmwork, the construction of living quarters, and our moves from place to place; but like recurrent malaria, it was a disease that never stopped plaguing our bodies. Records of "Labor" and "Leisure," or of this and that, are but mere adornments to this larger backdrop, minor incidents in a major story.

[1]"Downunder," of course, refers to Australia/New Zealand in English. Here it stands for the term *xiafang* (下放), literally "downward transfer." It applies more piognantly to the twenty million intellectuals uprooted from their academic and research institutions to live with the peasants in the countryside under military control during the Cultural Revolution.

[2]See note 6, p. 16.

All of this belongs to the past and the scene has now changed—we can say that many things have come to light. In this political campaign, as in all that preceded it, at least three types of people emerged. If the comrades who suffered under unjust accusations, who were criticized and "struggled against," were to write an account of this campaign, they might title it "A Record of Grievances" or "A Record of Resentment." As to the masses in general, in reminiscing, they might feel constrained to call theirs "A Record of Shame." This sense of shame and remorse could have its roots in their stupid inability to spot trumped-up charges or misjudged cases, which led them blindly to follow the crowd in trampling on decent people. Or perhaps they would be like me, feeling ashamed of their own cowardice, people who lacked the courage to protest that which they believed unjust, but whose most courageous act was "passive" participation in the campaign. The third type of person persisted in serving as flag-wavers, drum-beaters, and "hit-men" in helping to "settle" case after case in the "kangaroo courts,"[3] even though they knew full well that things were always messy and tangled-up, never clear-cut. These people should logically have the greatest need to write "A Record of Shame," but quite likely they have no recollection of what they did and feel no remorse over it. They may have forgotten the past precisely because of a sense of shame, or because they are impervious to shame. Shame often aids forgetfulness; in-

[3]"Kangaroo courts," used here to translate *hu-lu an* (葫蘆案), or a "bottle-gourd case," is a homonym for *hu-tu an* (糊塗案), a misjudged case, a miscarriage of justice, a "bum rap." The idiom *hu-lu*, for *hu-tu*, was current as early as Song and Yuan times, and often found in songs and dramas.

cidents that weigh on one's conscience or are disgraceful are never any fun to recall, so they easily slip through our minds and vanish without a trace. Shame also causes a person to recoil and hesitate, thus retarding his chances in a desperate struggle for survival. People with guilty consciences could, because of a momentary retreat from confrontation, place themselves forever in the ranks of stragglers. That is why shame is an emotion that must be eliminated, not nurtured, and why it is not included among the "seven human emotions"[4] listed in the ancient classics. As life in today's society grows increasingly tense, this state of mind is more than useless—it is harmful. So it is best forgotten in the interest of one's physical and mental well-being.

Six Chapters of a Floating Life—a book I never did like—actually only contains four extant chapters, while *Six Chapters from My Life "Downunder"* should theoretically have been seven. In this day and age, where collectors, antiquarians, and scholars combine their talents and interests, the discovery of unwritten or unpublished manuscripts by authors great and small has rapidly developed into a new field of literary endeavor. So who can say that the day will not come when the missing chapters of these two books will surface to fill in the gaps, thereby lessening somewhat the number of defects in the world of man.

Qian Zhongshu
December 1980

---

[4]They are: joy, anger, sorrow, fear, love, hate, and desire.

Farewell:
Departing for "Downunder"

I

IN FORMER DAYS the Chinese Academy of Social Sciences was called the Philosophy and Social Sciences Study Division of the Chinese Academy of Sciences—Study Division for short. My husband and I were assigned to the Study Division, Mo-cun[1] with the Institute of Literature and me with the Institute of Foreign Literature. In 1969 all intellectuals assigned to the Study Division began undergoing "re-education" with members of the Workers and PLA Propaganda Teams. In a shift toward "centralization" we were initially required to move into our offices, with as few

[1]Mo-cun 默存, the courtesy name (*zi* 字) of Qian Zhongshu (Ch'ien Chung-shu 錢鍾書), the author's husband.

as six or seven and as many as nine or ten people living in one room. We started off bright and early every morning with calisthenics, then sat through three separate study sessions: one in the morning, one in the afternoon, and one after dinner. Eventually the elderly and sickly were excused to return to their homes, while the study sessions dwindled to two—mornings and afternoons. So my husband and I moved back home, although we were aware that our days together were numbered and that we would soon be sent to a cadre school "downunder." The location of the cadre school was gradually narrowed down amidst a spate of rumors, but we could do nothing except guess the date of our departure—guess and wait.

Each day my husband and I lined up at our respective units' canteens to buy our lunches. It was always a wait of at least a half hour, but it would have been too much trouble to return home and cook a meal; besides, there wasn't enough time anyway. As time went by, the Workers and PLA Propaganda Teams relaxed their controls somewhat, so that most of the time the two of us could meet for lunch in the restaurants. The food there was certainly nothing to get excited about, but the wait afforded us the chance to exchange a few words.

On the third of November of that year I got off work at the Study Division and waited for my bus at the main entrance. While I was standing there I spotted Mo-cun emerging from a crowd of people and walking toward me. When he had drawn up alongside me he whispered: "I have something important to tell you." The look on his face gave no indication of what it was he wanted to say. After we had crowded onto the bus he finally told me:

"I'll be leaving on the eleventh. I'm part of the advance party."

Even though we had been expecting to be told any day when we would depart, the words still hit my ears like a clap of thunder. In a few days Mo-cun would be sixty years old (in Chinese reckoning), and we were planning to celebrate his birthday with a meal of longevity noodles. We had no illusions that we'd still be around to celebrate the seventieth. Now so few days remained, and before this birthday rolled around he'd be on his way down to the cadre school.

"Why do you have to be in the advance party?"

"Because of you. Others have to take their families with them or put things at home in order before they can go. But I can turn everything over to you."

The cadre school was located in Henan, in a place called Luoshan (Mt. Luo). The main party from Mo-cun's institute was scheduled to leave on the seventeenth.

We arrived at the little restaurant we had chosen, where we ordered the special of the day, a chicken casserole, which in fact contained nothing but skin and bones. I ladled out some of the clear broth and poured it over a half bowl of rice, but it didn't help my appetite.

We only had a week to get his luggage in order, and he had to work right up until the last two days. I used this as an excuse to take a few days off from the study sessions in order to get things ready around the house. This "downunder" assignment was supposed to be a "pots and pans" resettlement—we were to be uprooted from our homes and moved to the countryside, almost as though we would never return. Everything had to be taken—assorted useless objects, little-used clothing, prized books, notebooks, everything—until we had gathered quite a pile of belongings. We couldn't ask our daughter, A-yuan, and her husband, Deyi, to help us, since they weren't permitted to leave their factory jobs. But they did manage to come home on their day off, just in time to help us pack. They even tied the boxes and trunks up with thick cord the way they had seen other people do, to protect them against being crushed or otherwise damaged on the trip. Unfortunately, the only things the heavy cord could protect were the wooden boxes and heavy trunks, not human bodies, which seemed more capable of enduring rough treatment and abuse.

The euphemism for undergoing ill-treatment was "tempering" oneself, and getting ready for some "tempering" was about the only preparation we could make. Clothing was a problem: if it was too old, it would wear out easily, but if it was new and sturdy, washing it by hand would be difficult. I hadn't done any sewing for a long time, but I decided to sew a blanket cover out of some felt fabric that wouldn't show the dirt; that way it wouldn't have to be washed for years on end.

I mended a pair of Mo-cun's trousers, but when I had finished, the seat looked like a globe, with its crisscrossing lines of latitude and longitude, and the whole area was as thick as a tortoise shell. Mo-cun surprised me by saying how wonderful it was, just like carrying a cushion with him wherever he went—a built-in seat was just what he needed.

He remarked that I was making too big a fuss over all this, since I would be joining him soon and could look after him then. And then as soon as A-yuan and Deyi had settled in the countryside and the family was back together, the two of them could take care of us.

Before we knew it, the eleventh—the day of the advance party's departure—rolled around. A-yuan, Deyi, and I all went to see Mo-cun off. Since he didn't have many things with him, we searched out a quiet corner to rest before he had to board the train. The station waiting room was sheer chaos, with people noisily coming and going. The leaders of the advance party were so busy that they wished they could be twins, and the people who had too many bags to carry would have given anything to be blessed with extra pairs of hands. Deyi quickly put down the things he was holding and ran over to assist those who had more than they could handle. Seeing the enthusiasm with which our son-in-law offered his services to others, Mo-cun and I were moved to praise the direction the new society was taking. At the same time we reminded ourselves of our good fortune that A-yuan had a gentle, sincere man like Deyi.

While Deyi was lugging other people's belongings up to the platform, A-yuan and I helped Mo-cun with his few parcels as he joined the line. Once we boarded the train and got him settled into one of the cars, the three of us returned to the platform to wait stolidly for the train to pull out of the station.

Just then I recalled an earlier time when I had gone to see some people off on an ocean voyage. While they were still on the small ferryboat that would take them to the ocean liner, their friends and families had wished them bon voyage by throwing gaily colored streamers to them as the ferryboat pulled slowly away from the pier. One by one the streamers had stretched taut then snapped in two, as the well-wishers on the shore clapped and shouted. There had been some who did so tearfully, the snapped streamers betokening the sorrows of parting. But if the sorrows of parting between the cadre-school advance party and their friends and relatives on the platform who were seeing them off were observable, unlike the streamers, they were not gaily colored, nor could they be severed just like that.[2]

Mo-cun came up to the door and told us to go back home—waiting served no purpose. We looked at each other across the distance without uttering a word. The three of us assumed that it would put his mind at ease to see us walk off together rather than let him see in our eyes how disturbed his lone departure made us as the train built up speed, so we did as he asked, walking off without waiting for the train to pull out. We looked back several times to see that the train was still in the station and that the platform was still jammed with people. After walking me home in silence, A-yuan and Deyi returned to their factories. They worked in different factories, for even though they were at the same university, they belonged to different departments.

A couple of days later someone from the Institute of Literature informed me that it was all right to take one's

---

[2]Here the author adapts a well-known lyric by Li Yu (937-978), "Last Emperor" of the Southern Tang dynasty. The original lines read: 剪不斷，理還亂，是離愁，別是一般滋味在心頭。 Rendered loosely, the lyric should read as follows:
Cut it, and it severs not,
Comb it, and it remains a knot.
'Tis the sorrow of parting.
Yet another kind of flavor in the heart.

own bed to the cadre school, provided that it was tied securely with cord and delivered to the Study Division at once. It had to be tied securely with stiff, thick cord, and since it couldn't be knotted at either end, the ends had to be tucked tightly under the cord. This procedure normally required the efforts of at least two people, but since it had to be completed within twenty-four hours and I was all alone, I took a day off and dismantled our little bed all by myself. But no matter how hard I tried, I simply could not tie it all up together, so I had to do it in sections, and even that required another pair of hands to do it right. That, of course, was out of the question, so I did the best I could by using my teeth and hands to tie up the ends of the cord with thin twine, until I finally had the bed secured in three sections. Then I wrote Mo-cun's name on each of the sections. That little bed of ours in its dismantled state reminded me of a family during a time of war who was fearful that the moment they left their home they would be scattered to the four winds, never to be reunited. But in one of his letters, Mo-cun wrote that the three sections arrived intact, even though he had had to look high and low before they were all safely in his possession.

The Institute of Literature was one of the first two groups to depart for "downunder." Since military terminology was in vogue at the time, the word "company" replaced "institute." On the day that the first two "companies" departed for the countryside, all the rest of us in the Study Division put aside our work and gave them a grand send-off with gongs and drums. The departees closed up ranks, with the poet/scholar Yu Pingbo and his wife taking their place at the head of the column, and set out under the red flag. The sight of a revered scholar in his seventies who had to line up like a schoolchild to go to the cadre school was more than I could bear. I turned and headed home, discovering along the way that I wasn't the only one who lacked the customary enthusiasm for seeing someone off—many of my colleagues were drifting back to their places of work with blank looks on their faces.

As we awaited our turn to begin our "remolding" at the cadre school, we were in no mood to savor that "other kind of flavor."[3] For now that some members of the Study Division had already left for the cadre school, those of us who remained were hard put to get our work done. Virtually all we did, day in and day out, was to participate in study sessions, until even the "laborer-teachers" who were "reeducating" us were fed up with the situation. One young "laborer-teacher," who was twenty-two or twenty-three years old, grumbled: "I work all day long in front of a blast furnace tempering steel without feeling the least bit tired, but after sitting here all day, not only do I get a sore butt, but I'm beat to my socks." Obviously, tempering people is more exhausting work than tempering steel, and being a teacher[4] isn't all it's cracked up to be.

Tempering people was also a physical process—it involved manual labor. After we had finished constructing an air raid shelter—an underground structure that extended out in all directions—we started moving books back and forth. They had to be tied up into bundles before being carried from one building to another and one location to the next.

[3]See note 2.

[4]Literally, "sitting on a cold bench."

Then as soon as we had finished moving our unit's books, we had to give the other units a hand with theirs.

On one occasion we were told to clear the books, bookcases, and bookshelves out of a storage room that had been gathering dust for three years. As soon as we entered the room, one fellow began to sneeze from all the dust and didn't stop until he had sneezed twenty-odd times. We all covered our mouths and noses with makeshift masks, but when we emerged from the room our faces were still thick with dust and our spittle was black. The weather had just then turned hot, and all of those heavy metal bookshelves, huge bookcases, and bulky cabinets whose drawers were literally crammed full of index cards had to be carried out laboriously on the shoulders of young men. The heavily weighted carrying poles tore mercilessly into their clothing and exposed their skin. I marvelled at this sight—flesh and blood are still more likely to withstand abuse than anything else.

Being weak put me at an advantage, for I was assigned nothing but less demanding tasks. So whenever I had the time, I wrapped and mailed small parcels to Mo-cun, who wrote me letters during his spare time, managing a few sentences when he could at intermittent periods, day and night. If only we could have saved those letters, I'm sure they'd have made for interesting reading today. But what chance of survival did they have, when even all our important correspondence was destroyed!

When the advance party first arrived at the site, everyone had to man a broom to clean up a dirty, dusty old labor-reform camp. During the nights, which were still hot, the men slept on grass mats. Then a sudden snowstorm hit, turning the ground into a quagmire and chilling the night air. Once the main party arrived on the seventeenth, eighty unaccompanied men were crowded into a single room, where they all slept on earthen *kangs*. Among them was a mischievous boy who had been sent "downunder" with his father and who often ran around urinating on the *kangs* just before bedtime—"fertilizing" the sleeping men, so to speak.

The men went into town on their days off to buy food, things like roast chicken and cooked tortoise. I asked Mo-cun about the tortoise meat, but he said he hadn't tasted any of it, though he secretly composed some limericks on the subject, which he then sent to me.[5]

There was no arable land in Luoshan and no useful work to perform at the cadre school. So after staying there a little more than a month, everyone was ordered to gather family and belongings together and move en masse to a place in Xi County called Dongyue. Xi County was listed on the map, but not Dongyue. It was a place with poor land and even poorer people. Since there was no firewood to heat the furnaces during the winter, many of the female comrades developed chilblains on their faces. To do their washing they had to squat alongside the pond and pound the clothes with a club; Mo-cun asked one of the local women to wash one of his new shirts, which he never saw again. Since I was more concerned about his falling into the pond than losing his shirt, I wouldn't have minded losing a few more so long as he could get someone to wash his clothes.

---

[5]Since to the Chinese the tortoise represents "cuckoldry," the nature and tone of these limericks can easily be imagined.

The people in Peking who were waiting to be resettled were understandably concerned about life at the cadre school, so they often asked me to tell them what I knew. Their favorite story was the one about the poet He Qifang and the fish. It seems that the locals had drained the pond to get at the fish, which temporarily improved the quality of food in the dining hall—braised fish suddenly appeared on the menu. Comrade He rushed over with the mug he used for rinsing his mouth to buy a portion for himself. But he discovered that it had a funny taste, which got worse with each bite, so he scooped out the largest piece of fish to see just what was wrong. What he found was some undissolved medicinal soap, which he had forgotten to remove from the mug before filling it with the fish. The story was always met with raucous laughter mixed with a considerable measure of sympathy.

Then it was someone else's turn to tell me a humorous incident. It seems that Qian Zhongshu and a Mr. Ding, who also held the rank of senior researcher, were unable to bring a cauldron of water to a boil, no matter how long they worked at it. I jumped to their defense, saying that the furnace was out in the open, where it was at the mercy of the wind and snow, and boiling a cauldron of water was no easy task. But a funny story is still a funny story.

After the first of the year, the residents began building their own dwellings. The female comrades did their share of hauling carts, making adobe blocks and bricks, and actually building the houses, thus serving as a part of the hard-working labor force. Mo-cun, Yu Pingbo, and several others of the "old, weak, sick, and disabled" contingent, who were excused from participating in this labor, had only a few light duties to perform.

Our company didn't leave for "downunder" until the others had been there for eight months. By then they had already moved into their newly-built houses. We departed for the cadre school on July 12, 1970. On that earlier occasion, there had been three of us to see Mo-cun off—A-yuan, Deyi, and myself. But this time A-yuan was there alone to see me off—Deyi had taken his own life a month earlier.

My son-in-law had been the first to admit that he was somewhat of a "right-leaner," but he simply could not abide that bunch of ultra-leftists. When the campaign to root out the "May Sixteenth" elements[6] began at the university, several ultra-leftists who were suspected of having "May Sixteenth" tendencies got together to accuse Deyi of being their "organizer," saying that the "May Sixteenth" roster was in his possession. He had by then already returned to the university, leaving A-yuan behind to continue working in the factory, since they were not permitted to return together. As he was leaving me for what turned out to be the last time, he said: "Mama, I can't have a bad attitude toward the masses, nor can I talk back to the Propaganda Team, but that doesn't mean that I'm prepared to fabricate a roster and get other people into trouble. And I'm not about to start lying!" When he arrived at the university, he was placed in detention. Class struggle was just then spreading like wildfire, so A-yuan and the other workers at her factory were sent back to the university, where the Propaganda Team leaders forced them to "struggle" against Deyi three times a day,

[6]A radical Maoist group who came under attack during the Cultural Revolution for anarchistic and nihilistic tendencies.

demanding that he produce the roster. He responded by committing suicide.

After A-yuan saw me onto the train, I urged her to go back home and not wait for the train to pull out. There was really no reason to worry about leaving her behind, since she was anything but a delicate little girl, but the sight of her walking off alone pained me deeply, and I quickly closed my eyes. All that accomplished was to produce a scene in my mind's eye of her all alone trying to straighten up our run-down, messy house. I hurriedly opened my eyes and looked out the window, but she was gone, so I closed my eyes again, this time to keep the tears from running down my cheeks. The train moved slowly out of the station and took me away from Peking.

The Mo-cun I saw at the cadre school was deeply tanned and very thin—he had changed so much it was a wonder that I could recognize him at all.

The doctor assigned to the cadre school was a no-nonsense, outspoken woman named Huang. Mo-cun visited her once with a medical problem, and when she noticed that he had signed the register with the name Qian Zhongshu, she reacted angrily: "What are you trying to pull! What do you mean by calling yourself Qian Zhongshu! I know Qian Zhongshu personally!" Mo-cun insisted that he was Qian Zhongshu, to which Dr. Huang responded: "I know Qian Zhongshu's wife." Mo-cun rose to the challenge by telling her my name. Dr. Huang still wasn't entirely convinced, but since it didn't really make any difference whether Mo-cun was passing himself off as someone else or not, the discussion came to an end. Some time later I reminded Dr. Huang of this incident, to which she responded with a laugh: "So what—he didn't look anything like himself."

I can no longer recall exactly what Mo-cun looked like then, nor what he was wearing. All I remember is that there was a red lump below and to the right of his chin. It had an angry, threatening look about it, even though it was no larger than a hazelnut. The head was a shiny red, while the color at the base was dark yellow, a sure sign that it was filled with pus. "Aiya!" I blurted out in alarm. "Is that a carbuncle? You need some hot compresses." But who was going to prepare them for him? I spotted a Red Cross first-aid kit, only to discover that the gauze and absorbent cotton were covered with grimy fingerprints. Mo-cun told me that this wasn't the first time he had had a skin eruption, and that the leaders had given him a few days off before relieving him of his duties of boiling water and giving him a new assignment. He was now in charge of watching over the tools during the day and was a roving patrolman at night.

His immediate superior gave him a half day off so that we could be together, but my platoon commander, a hard-nosed disciplinarian, would only let me go over and see him briefly with a chaperone, ordering me to return to my unit immediately afterwards. Mo-cun walked me back to my unit, where we parted, having spoken no more than a few words. Since A-yuan and I had decided to withhold the news of Deyi's death from him for the moment, I avoided the subject. A couple of days later he wrote to tell me that the lump had indeed been a carbuncle, which had developed five perforations. Fortunately, the condition gradually cleared up after a few injections.

It only took an hour or so for one of us to go see the other, but we each had our orders, which we had to follow to the letter. Discipline was to be vigorously maintained, and we weren't free to go anywhere we wanted. So we normally stayed in touch by writing letters, with personal visits limited to our days off. And that didn't necessarily mean Sundays, since we were given a day off only once every ten days—it was called an "extended Sunday"—and even that could be cancelled if there was work to do. But compared to A-yuan, who was all alone in Peking, we considered ourselves as being together.

Labor: Digging a Well

II

THERE WERE many forms of manual labor at the cadre school, including farmwork like planting beans and wheat. During the dog days of summer, the field hands had to be at their jobs by three in the morning, on empty stomachs. Their breakfast was sent out to them at six, which they paused to eat before going back to work. They knocked off at noon to rest while the sun was at its peak, then at dusk they were back in the fields, not quitting until late at night.

As each new company arrived, the people were temporarily housed with local villagers, but the first order of business was to start work on their own living quarters. They should have had bricks to build their houses, but since bricks were so hard to come by, more often than not adobe blocks were used as a substitute. Making these blocks was one of the hardest jobs around, while tending pigs was the dirtiest and most disagreeable work of all. Most of the garden and kitchen duties were reserved for the weak and elderly, which placed the responsibility for all the strenuous labor on the shoulders of the young.

On one occasion, the school authorities held a big celebration for something or other, at which the entire program dealt with some aspect of labor. There was a dramatic skit about a "student" from a certain company who was undaunted by the prospect of his brick kiln caving in on top of him, risking his neck to turn out more and more bricks. It was supposedly based upon an actual incident. Another company performed a skit about digging a well. Although the stage was packed with actors, there wasn't a single line of dialogue, and the only action consisted of the entire "troupe" pushing the well-boring machine round and round and round. They kept up their cadence with a constant rhythmical "Heave-ho! Heave-ho! Heave-ho! Heave-ho!" Meanwhile, they negotiated one revolution after another with never so much as a pause. This was their way of showing that once the digging began, there was no stopping until the well came in. "Heave-ho! Heave-ho! Heave-ho! Heave-ho!" The deep, heavy sound never varied, calling to mind the movie *Song of the Volga Boatmen*, which had once enjoyed some popularity. I could almost picture a gang of boatpullers as they inched forward, step by step, on the banks of a river, straining against the almost inhuman forces their exhausted bodies were being subjected to. Admittedly, it was a monotonous presentation, but one that impressed me as more moving and more realistic than the skit glorifying the kiln worker who feared neither hardship nor death. When the gathering broke up, we all discussed this particular skit, praising it for its effects and commenting on the naturalness of the production—all they had had to do was mount the stage and the show was on, no rehearsals needed.

But then someone blurted out: "*Aiya!* That skit... didn't seem quite right, ideology-wise,[7] did it? It's as if...as if...we're all so...so..." The humor was not lost on us, and there was a round of laughter. That was followed by a brief silence, after which we started talking about other things.

I was assigned to the vegetable-plot detail. Without the benefit of any machinery, and relying solely on the sweat of our own brows, we had to dig a small well for ourselves.

Fortune had smiled on our cadre school, for the area on the banks of the Huai River had experienced two arid years in a row, and we were never visited by floods. But the other side of the coin was the difficulty of planting anything in the rock-hard earth. The people had a saying about the soil in Xi County: "When it rains, the ground's a morass; when the sun comes out, it's as hard as brass." After we ran the plow over the vegetable plot, the entire area was covered with dirt clods the size of human heads

[7]The absence of a central heroic figure could be considered contrary to Jiang Qing's demand for positive proletarian figures in all literary and dramatic works. See Background Notes, p.106

.id harder than bone. Before we could do any planting, we had to level the soil, which meant crumbling up every single clod—not only was it back-breaking work, but it sorely tried our patience as well.

After levelling the soil, we dug a series of irrigation ditches, only to discover that there was no water. The neighboring plot, which also belonged to the Study Division cadre school, had a mechanized well that, we were told, was some ten meters deep. We often went over there to get our drinking water, since our hand-dug well was no more than three meters deep and produced muddy water. Boiling the water before we drank it was out of the question, so we added a small vial of patent medicine to each bucketful, which we hoped would make it potable. This gave our water a funny taste, while the water from the ten-meter well was so cool and sweet that drinking a cupful under the glaring sun was like being blessed with manna from Heaven. We didn't stop at drinking the water, either; we even washed up in it. The difficulty arose when we tried to use it to irrigate the crops, for without a pump, it was impossible to transport the water from the well to the field. Somehow we managed to borrow a pump, which we put to use at once. But not long after the water began running through the ditches we had dug and had irrigated a few of the parcels, night fell and the pump was retrieved by its owners.

We covered one section of the plot with spinach seeds, but it wasn't until a month later, after a heavy rainfall, that we finally saw some green sprouts. We decided then and there that we had to have a well to irrigate our own crops, so we selected the location, broke ground, and started right to work.

The soil in that particular spot was so hard it was like trying to wear away a hunk of brass with nothing but the wind. I worked with every ounce of energy I could muster, gouging at the earth with a spade, but the only result was a solitary scratch on the surface. The youngsters around me had quite a laugh over that. But they still threw themselves into their work, even though they said they needed pointed shovels. Since my "long suit" was a quickness of foot, and since I wasn't getting anywhere with my spade, I ran like the wind back to the company area, where I fetched two pointed shovels, rested them on my shoulder, and, much to even my own surprise, ran like the wind back to the vegetable plot. The others never let up with their hands; I never let up with my feet.

By spreading the work around, the hard crust of the earth finally gave in to the relentless assaults by the shovels and started to crumble, at which time the rest of us began to dig into the soil. Finally, after a day of unremitting toil, we managed to scoop out a deep pit, even though it was dry as a bone.

The youngster we called "Little Ox" was a real male chauvinist; he mumbled that there was no place for women in well-digging, that water wouldn't make an appearance as long as there were women around. Now, there were only two women assigned to the vegetable-plot detail, including me, and I was the oldest woman in our entire company; the other woman, A-xiang, was the youngest in the company—she was perhaps half my age. She was a returned overseas Chinese who, upon overhearing a comment like this for the first time in her life, was both enraged and amused. She relayed the comment to me with a chuckle, then walked over to "Little Ox" to engage him in debate and register a strong protest.

The truth of the matter was that she and I were a little apprehensive, for if by some chance we dug in the wrong spot and came up dry, the others might hold us responsible. Fortunately, by the time we were two meters down, the soil turned damp and water came into view.

Difficult though it had been to dig in the hardbaked soil, working in the mud at the lower depths was, if anything, even more trying. And it got worse the deeper we dug. Two or three men jumped barefoot into the pit and continued to dig, hoisting bucketful after bucketful of heavy mud up to the others, who dumped it off to the side. In no time at all, a wall of mud girded the rim of the wellsite. By then, everyone had shed shoes and socks, including A-xiang, who worked spiritedly in this barefoot bucket brigade. Although the buckets were too heavy for me to lift, I got into the spirit of the work, taking off my shoes and socks and using my shovel to level off the gooey mud that was being dumped all over the place.

I had always felt that mud was a terribly dirty substance, full of spit, snot, feces, and urine. But the effect of having it ooze up through my toes was a feeling of intimacy with the soil; I saw it as something slippery—almost creamy— rather than something dirty from which I wanted to shy away. It was almost like having a loved one with a contagious disease: the disease, rather than inducing loathing, becomes an acceptable part of the loved one. I had to laugh at myself: could this be an indication that my views were undergoing a change, that I was gaining a new "foothold?"

We were concerned that the digging would be interrupted when the water started to gush upward, so although digging a well by hand cannot proceed day and night until the job is completed, as it can with a mechanized well digger, we knew we had to keep at it for as long as we could. That was why we did as the workers on the big farms: we got up very early in the morning and went to work at the vegetable plot on empty stomachs. At breakfast time A-xiang and I went back to the kitchen to pick up the steamed buns, congee, pickled vegetables, boiled water, and whatever else they had prepared, then placed it all on a cart and delivered it to the workers at the vegetable plot. It was my job to push the cart on the even stretches of road and down the inclines, while A-xiang took over wherever the road bent or twisted and up all the hills. She had a tough job: if she lost control—even a little—she ran the risk of spilling the congee and boiled water on the ground. I tried it myself and I know what I'm talking about. Fortunately, this unequal division of labor didn't bother my young and hardy partner, and the arrangement suited the two of us just fine. Everyone went back to the company area at noontime to rest before returning to the fields to continue our work until dusk. We were always the last to sit down to dinner.

I forget just how many days of back-breaking labor it took us to dig to a depth of three meters, but during the last few days, as the amount of water standing in what was going to be our well increased, we found the going harder and harder. Finally we were forced to seek outside help in the form of two strapping young men. By then, anyone who went down into the pit found himself standing in a pool of water. Wells are generally dug in the winter, when the water at the bottom is nice and warm; but we were digging in the heat of mid-summer, when the water at the bottom was cold and raw. Both A-xiang and I were worried that the men would catch their death of cold from standing in the chilly water, but they were warmed by their own enthusiasm and high spirits—there wasn't a single complaint of the cold. Since neither of us wanted to appear too motherly, we had to be content with standing at the edge of the well and keeping our eyes peeled for any problems.

The water level slowly rose until it covered their knees, then their thighs, and eventually their waists. We could see that three meters was going to be deep enough for our purposes. I volunteered to buy a catty of strong liquor, with which the workers could take the edge off the chill and with which we could all celebrate our little victory. My offer was met with total approval. One of the men who had come to help us was a logistics team leader, who gave me a suggestion on how to go about getting my hands on some liquor. So I went back to the company kitchen with the story I had been coached to give the cooks in order to borrow their liquor bottle. Evidently, they were on the lookout for pilferage, since the word "poison," followed by three exclamation marks, had been affixed to the bottle; further emphasis had been added by a skull and crossbones beneath the label. Only about an inch of liquor remained in the bottle.

I hugged the frightful bottle close to me and lit out for Central Supply, which was less than a mile west of the vegetable plot. That's where I was going to have to get the liquor. I couldn't shake the fear that by the time I got to the co-op it would be closed; what I wouldn't have given to have had the use of the Magic Messenger's leggings then![8] Since I had no liquor ration card I had to show them the bottle and talk a blue streak before I was allowed to buy a catty of liquor. The only thing they had to go with it was some candy that was as hard as a rock, so I bought a catty of that and hurried back to the vegetable plot.

The well—our source of irrigation—was finished, so all of us—those who had done either the hard work or the lighter jobs—sat down on the ground and rested as we excitedly filled water glasses of every size and description with the liquor I had brought. We nearly finished off the full catty, leaving an inch or so in the bottle to return to the kitchen. The rock candy vanished without a trace, and that was our victory feast for a job well done.

There was no way I could tell just how taxing all that work had been, but the moans and groans from my roommates as they tossed and turned in their sleep after a hard day's work was a pretty good indication, and the personal shame I experienced made for many sleepless nights. I imagined that these women must have ached all over. I even heard some of the young men complain that they were "feeling very, very old" and were troubled by the fact that they had lost the vigor and stamina they had had in their twenties. They must have come to the painful realization that their will to work now exceeded their own abilities.

[8]A character named Dai Zong in the classical novel *Shuihu zhuan* (Men of the Marshes), who could cover 800 *li* in one day with the aid of magic leggings.

By the time we had a pulley in place, the water in the well was overflowing. Given the broad mouth of the well, the circumference of the platform around it was so great that we had to outfit it with a long horizontal bar in order to lower the machinery into the water. It turned out to be a blessing in disguise, for the wide sweeps we had to make as we walked round the well turning the machinery lessened the possiblility of our getting dizzy. The younger ones in our group put their strength and stamina to the test by seeing how many revolutions they could make without taking a break or being spelled by someone else. Some of them managed as many as a hundred. Even the people who had come over to give us a hand admitted that constantly stooping over to work in the vegetable plot was hard work, as was turning the pulley at the well.

Although the various light tasks I performed didn't make me one of the "laborers," I joined the others every day as they went to work early and returned late. Just being with them gave me a sense of participation, until I began to get a feeling of what they call the "collective spirit" or "camaraderie." It seemed perfectly natural for me to speak in terms of "us" and "we";[9] I guess you could say that I truly felt that I "belonged." This sort of feeling seldom results from a short-termed group-labor project in which everyone goes his own way as soon as the job is done. Mental labors do not readily lend themselves to this sort of concerted effort—people can cooperate, but it is more a matter of contributing individual achievements

[9]Here the author uses both the all-inclusive term for "us" or "we," *women*, and the more restrictive *zamen*, which includes only the speaker and those spoken to; thus the use of "us" and "we" in the translation is intended to carry the tone.

than of working as a team with a single purpose. When people collaborate on an article, for instance, it is virtually impossible for those who gather the material and those who actually do the writing to feel that they are two fingers from the same hand working together toward a common goal. But after months and months of manual labor at the cadre school, with no other prospects in sight, a "group mentality" gradually took over.

I heard people from the cadre school say things like: "After all, they don't know what it's like to slosh around in the rain or work under the glaring sun." "They," mind you! You see, there was not one great, homogeneous "we" among all the companies who made up the labor force, including those who had spent time locked up in the infamous "cow sheds."[10] Those who controlled our lives were generally referred to as "them." But that doesn't mean that every one who directed our activities belonged to the "them" category, any more than all those who "didn't know what it was like to slosh around in the rain or work under the glaring sun" did. One of our supervisors, a man who put on great airs of leadership and treated his subordinates with perfunctory disdain, was the typical "them." But he wasn't the only one—there were the "ass-kissers," the "damned national treasures," and others of their ilk, who were just as typical. The difference between "us" and "them" wasn't the same as class distinction, but the experience I gained from participating in collective labor had an enlightening effect on me: I drew closer to grasping the meaning of "class sympathies."

[10]Places of temporary detention for persons attacked in the Cultural Revolution.

We "students" at the cadre school were viewed as outsiders by the people we called our teachers—the poor and lower-middle peasants. Countless mounds of sweet potatoes that we had planted were dug up and stolen in a single night, and virtually all the vegetables we planted were similarly stolen as soon as they were ready to be picked. What the peasants said was: "You buy your food every day, so why do you have to plant your own crops?" They dug up all the saplings we planted, then turned around and sold them in the market-place. When it was time for us to harvest our soybeans, not only did they come out and grab them right out from under our noses, they even justified their actions with comments like: "You can buy all the grain you need from the stores!" To them we were anything but part of "us"; they referred to us as "ill-clad, well-fed people with wrist-watches"—in other words, "them."

Leisure: Tending a Vegetable Plot

III

EVERY MEMBER of our company was a hard worker and a hearty eater—I guess we might call this a case of "from each according to his ability, to each according to his needs." Of course, this doesn't tell the whole story, since not everyone received the same wages. I didn't eat much, had little strength, and performed only light tasks, but I was paid a very high wage. I guess this could be characterized as taking full advantage of the "superiority of socialism," even though the cost to the nation was considerable. I felt rather awkward about this situation, but no one took my discomfort seriously. So I just toed the line, going about my business of planting vegetables at the cadre school.

There is a great deal of work involved in starting a new vegetable plot. First on the list of things to do is building a toilet. Since we were counting on gathering a good part of our fertilizer supply from passersby, we chose a site just off the roadway on the northern edge of the farm. We erected five wooden posts—one for each corner and an additional one on the side where the door would go—then made walls out of woven sorghum stalks, and that took care of the enclosure. Inside we buried a large earthen compost basin; in front of that we dug two shallow holes into which we fitted bricks for footrests. That completed our toilet. The only thing we needed now was some sort of curtain for the door. A-xiang and I decided that it should be as neat and clean a curtain as we could make. We settled on the smooth core of sorghum stalks from which we had stripped the outer layer; we then wove them closely and neatly together with hempen cord, resulting in as lovely a door curtain as one could imagine, which we proudly hung in front of the door of what was now a quite unique toilet. We were shocked, to say the least, when we came out early the next morning and discovered that not only had our door curtain disappeared, but that even the accumulated compost had been stolen. From that day onward, A-xiang and I had to serve as one another's "door curtain" whenever we used the toilet.

Our vegetable plot was not an enclosed area—to the west, south, and southwest it bordered on three other vegetable plots that also belonged to the Study Division cadre school. One of them possessed a toilet of such sophistication that all the waste material ran into a detached cesspool, and the hole inside was enclosed by bricks. But most of the compost in that toilet was similarly pilfered, for local wisdom had it that the waste produced in the cadre school was the best around.

We dug a shallow rectangular pit to produce green manure. Then we all went out and cut down large quantities of grass, which we laid in the pit; but in about as much time as it takes to eat a meal, the grass that was steeping in the pit disappeared as if on wings—it was probably put to use as feed for oxen. Grass was in such short supply there that dry grass—roots and all—was used in place of firewood.

The first companies to be sent downunder had constructed three- and five-room dwellings on the vegetable-plot site. We hurriedly erected a shed for ourselves on the northwestern edge of the well, first throwing up a wooden framework, then forming a rammed-earth wall on the northern side. The other three sides were closed in with woven sorghum stalks, which also went to make up the roof, on top of which we added a layer of asphalt felt and sheets of plastic for insulation. A brick kiln belonging to the Study Division cadre school was located just northwest of the vegetable plot; the ground around it was strewn with broken bricks. So we filled up two carts with cast-off bricks, with which we laid a floor in the shed to keep the inside from getting too damp. After all, people had to live there. Finally we hung a sturdy door in the southern wall and even outfitted it with a lock. Three people were assigned to live in the shed and keep watch over the vegetable plot: the leader of our unit, a poet who worked the plot with us, and "Little Ox." The shed also served as a resting place for the other workers.

One by one we planted seeds in each of the vegetable beds. Mostly we sowed Chinese cabbage and turnips, although we also planted small quantities of things like greens, leeks, potherb mustard, lettuce, carrots, coriander, and garlic. However, all the companies, with the exception of the first few to arrive downunder, had built their homes near the school's Central Compound, which was quite some distance from our plot. So we opened another plot near the newly constructed buildings; some of the stronger men levelled the ground and dug irrigation ditches. And since we couldn't leave the original plot unattended, A-xiang and I were assigned to keep watch there.

We took some Napa cabbages and wrapped them up leaf by leaf, tying each one with vine. Some of them actually grew to look like regular Chinese cabbage, although they weren't as tightly packed as the real thing. A-xiang had strength enough to carry two half-filled buckets of urine on a carrying pole, but I was only able to irrigate the fields a cupful at a time. Our favorite crops were the "ivory turnips" or "Taihu turnips," which were actually long white things. Their tips, which were the size of a ricebowl, only stuck up out of the ground an inch or so. "What we're raising here is the cream of the crop," we confided to one another. So we used all of the plant ash our unit leader had told us to spread among the carrots to fertilze our little darlings instead. And what darlings they were! When it came time to harvest our "crop" I was certain that the ground would yield up turnips a foot or more in length, or at the very least half that long. I planted my feet on the ground and tugged for all I was worth, so hard, in fact, that I lost my balance and plopped unceremoniously onto the ground. That was because beneath the surface there were only a few skinny tassels. That was the first time I'd ever seen a "long" turnip *that* flat! Some of the radishes we grew didn't look too bad, although they were no larger than "duck pears."

Then the weather began to turn cold. As we squatted in the vegetable beds pulling weeds, the cold north winds penetrated our clothing. It was invariably dark by the time we returned to the company area to eat dinner. By that December all of the new homes had been completed, so the entire company moved into the Central Compound, and A-xiang was assigned to work in the new vegetable plot. The three people who shared the shed now returned to the old plot to sleep each night, so that during the days I kept a solitary watch.

The unit leader had given me this assignment for my own good; since Mo-cun's dormitory was located a short distance to the north of the brick kiln, it only took me a little more than ten minutes to walk there. Mo-cun had by then been placed in charge of the toolshed, so our unit leader often sent me over to borrow tools, which naturally had to be returned afterwards. My coworkers giggled like schoolgirls when they saw me walking over and back with unbridled enthusiasm as I borrowed tools and then returned them. Mo-cun's sole duty as the man in charge of tools was to register the names of users; and he also served as roving patrolman on a rotating basis. His official designation was mailman, a job that consisted of going to the post office in town every afternoon to pick up newspapers, letters, and parcels, then returning to camp and distributing them. The post office was southeast of our plot, and each afternoon Mo-cun followed the meandering stream to the south of our plot, first heading south then east. Sometimes he would skirt around the plot and come over to see me. Whenever he did that, we all stopped work and made him feel welcome. But he dared not spend too much time with us, and he seldom came by, so as to disrupt our schedule as little as possible. While A-xiang was sharing the lookout duties with me, she would sometimes nudge me suddenly and cry out: "Well, look here, look who's coming!" Mo-cun would be returning from the post office with a sackful of mail, heading straight toward the vegetable plot. The three of us would exchange greetings across the stream and chat for a moment or two. Later on, when I was alone in the plot, the stream had dried up to the point that one could jump across it, so Mo-cun no longer had to skirt the stream to get to the plot, but could cross it on his way to the post office. That afforded this old couple the chance to be together, a great improvement over the old Chinese novels and operas, where young lovers had to arrange their trysts in rear gardens.

Mo-cun eventually discovered that it was unnecessary for him to jump across the stream, since there was a stone bridge that would take him to the eastern bank on his way south. Every afternoon I could see him striding toward me as he headed over from the kiln off to the north. When the weather was nice, we often sat for a while on the bank of the irrigation ditch to the south of the shed and just soaked up the sun. Sometimes he came by so late that we barely had time to speak before he had to be on his way again.

But first he would hand me a letter in which he had jotted down bits and pieces as they had occurred to him the previous day. I often locked the door of the shed and walked him over to the stream, then rushed back to the vegetable plot to keep an eye on things. I would watch him walk off into the distance, growing smaller and smaller until he disappeared completely.

He didn't dare cross the stream to see me on his way back from the post office, since he was always in a hurry to get back to the unit to deliver his mail and newspapers. But I could still see him as he walked along the road in our direction, and if I had forgotten to tell him something earlier, I could always have a brief conversation with him across the stream as he passed by.

This vegetable plot was the center of my world. There was a mound of earth on the southwest border which the people referred to as "Tiger Mountain."[11] It was situated directly across from the brick kiln far off on the northwestern border. Mo-cun's dormitory was located a little ways to the north of the kiln. The Central Compound of the entire cadre school was a considerable distance to the west of Tiger Mountain—our unit's dormitory was on the southern edge of this compound. The dining hall belonging to one of the other units was located at the foot of Tiger Mountain, and that's where I went to buy my lunches and dinners. My drinking water I usually got from the people in the buildings on a neighboring vegetable plot to the west. Once in a while I asked for some boiled water

[11]An allusion to *Taking Tiger Mountain By Strategy*, one of the eight "model revolutionary operas" promoted by Jiang Qing during the Cultural Revolution.

from the people who had a stove in a shed south of ours. I had set up a small fireplace with only three bricks, in which I tried to boil water over a fire of dried sorghum stalks, but that was impossible in a strong wind. If I travelled south I could reach the post office where Mo-cun made his daily pickups of mail and newspapers. The area east of the stream was lush with green fields and flat fields as far as the eye could see; the few clusters of green trees off on the horizon belonged to the neighboring villages. A place called Yang Village, where I had once stayed, was located to the east of those trees. The vegetable plot was the center of my daily activity, and in that respect, I was like a spider who had settled there to spin a web all around her; several trifling observations and ephemeral emotions were trapped in this web of mine.

I set out alone for the vegetable plot every morning immediately after breakfast. On the road I often ran into the three people who slept in the shed as they headed toward the Central Compound to get their breakfast. When I arrived at my destination, the first thing I did was reach into the sorghum stalks alongside the door of the shed and fish out the key. After opening the door I'd put down the ricebowls and other odds and ends I'd brought along with me, then lock the door behind me and go out to take a look around the plot. Our carrot patch was at the eastern extremity, where the soil was so hard and barren that the harvests never came up to our expectations. The few carrots that did reach a respectable size were, as often as not, picked on the sly, and so hastily that the thieves snapped them off, leaving only stumps behind. I'd dig out the stumps, wash them off with well water, and save them to help quench my thirst later on. As for the Chinese cabbages planted alongside the nearby road to the north, no sooner were they plump and ready to be eaten than they would be picked and taken away, with only the newly severed stalks remaining in the soil. I once discovered three or four freshly cut stalks of fully grown cabbages on the ground, while the cabbages themselves, which had been left behind in the rush, were resting there in the vegetable bed as though nothing had happened. We knew we'd better pick the cabbages right away before they were fully grown.

On one occasion I walked around to the rear of the shed, where I caught three women in the act of stealing some of our greens right out of the ground. They got to their feet and ran off, never thinking that I'd take off after them. They tossed the greens away as they ran, and once their baskets were empty they were no longer frightened by the prospect that I'd catch them. Actually, I was chasing them only because I was expected to; I would have preferred to let them take the greens home and eat them, for my retrieving them served absolutely no purpose.

Those particular women had just been passing by. Normally, the villagers came out in groups of ten or so to pick kindling and various grasses. Their ages ran from seven or eight to twelve or thirteen, and there were both boys and girls among them. They would be led out of the village by a girl of sixteen or seventeen or perhaps by one of the older women of forty or fifty. Wearing brightly colored but tattered clothes, they would be carrying baskets over their arms and small knives or spades in their hands. When they reached a likely spot they'd split up into groups of two or three and start foraging around. If they came across something worth taking, into the basket it went. They didn't immediately pick up the twigs and branches they cut off the trees in the woods, nor did they necessarily put those they did pick into their baskets right away. They normally just stacked them in piles alongside the roads or on the banks of canals and tied them into bundles. Then when it was time for lunch or dinner they'd walk back home as a unit, the bundles of firewood and dried grass on their backs, and baskets full of whatever they had found on their arms. Some of the bolder boys even uprooted little saplings, which they also tied into bundles and tossed into a creek; these they retrieved before mealtime and carried home with them.

The sorghum stalks that had been more or less dumped all around the shed had long since been picked clean by these people; the five wooden posts used to construct the toilet had gradually dwindled to two, and before long they too were gone. Even the sorghum stalks on the toilet walls were getting noticeably thinner, a condition that gradually spread to the shed itself. I always waited until the people with bundles of firewood and grass on their backs had passed by and were a long way off before I'd dare to walk over to the dining hall at the foot of Tiger Mountain to buy my meal.

There was once a harvest of cabbages in the neighboring farm to the south of ours. They had more people than we and they were stronger; the quickness and agility with which they worked could not have been more different than ours. Our unit was composed mainly of older and weaker people. We chopped, we picked, we stacked the stuff into piles, which we then weighed, recorded, loaded into carts, and delivered to the kitchen in the Central Compound...We were busy the day long, and our vegetable beds were cluttered with the discarded outer leaves of the cabbages. But the other company had finished their harvest before sunset, leaving the fields swept completely clean of crop residue. An old woman and her daughter sat in front of our shed waiting to go out and pick the outer cabbage leaves. Every once in a while the girl would run over to see how things were going, then return and report on the progress of the harvest. Finally the old woman got to her feet and said: "Let's go!"

"They've swept it clean," the girl answered her.

They spoke so rapidly that I had trouble understanding them. About the only thing I picked up was "feed the pigs," which was repeated several times. The old woman muttered angrily: "Even the landlords allowed us to pick that!"

I asked them how they could eat the old outer leaves of the cabbages.

The girl answered by saying that they first boiled some water, into which they dumped the shredded leaves, then added flour paste and stirred it all together. "It really tastes good!"

I'd seen their steamed buns, which were reddish-brown in color, as was the flour paste they used. I wondered about the flavor of this flour paste that "really tastes good." The tough cabbage and bitter turnips that comprised our daily fare wasn't very tasty, but we never tried that stuff of theirs that "really tastes good," even though we should have.

We never really harvested the lump-vegetables we had planted. The big ones grew as large as peaches, while the smaller ones were no larger than almonds. I had gathered a pile, which I was sorting in order to deliver the large ones to the kitchen. The old woman, who sat off to the side staring at me the whole time, asked me how those were eaten. I told her they could be pickled or boiled. Then I said to her: "I'll keep the big ones and you can have the small ones." She was delighted, saying over and over: "Okay, you take the big ones and I'll take the small ones." But her hands were too quick for me, and she began stuffing her basket with the larger ones. Since I didn't want to cause a scene, I just waited until she had filled her basket, then relieved her of the biggest ones, swapping them for two handfuls of smaller ones. She offered no resistance and walked off very contented. But I later had cause to feel remorse over the whole incident, since the kitchen help never did use the pile of large lump-vegetables I had presented to them. At the time, however, I didn't dare give things away to anyone I pleased and was afraid to set a precedent.

Whenever I was weeding and pruning in the vegetable plot, some of the village girls would run over to watch me work. Once I had mastered their local speech I passed the time of day with them. I gave them some of the smaller twigs and they helped me do the weeding. They referred to their menfolk as "the big guys." They were all young girls of twelve or thirteen whose future marriages had been arranged by their parents. One of them told me that one of the others had already been accepted by her in-laws. This comment obviously embarrassed the girl referred to, who denied the charge and turned it right back to the first girl. Neither of them was literate. The family I had lived with for a while in another village was better off than the families of these girls; their two sons, who were in the neighborhood of ten years of age, didn't need to tend oxen to make a little money, but were both in school. Their seventeen- or eighteen-year-old sister, on the other hand, was illiterate. Her parents had enlisted the aid of a matchmaker, and the girl was already engaged to be married to a PLA soldier whose age and appearance were just right. The two of them had never laid eyes on one another, but the soldier had written his fiancée a letter and sent her a photograph. Both his level of education and his appearance were those of a simple farmer. The girl's family and I shared the same surname, so they called me "Auntie"; they asked me to write a letter for them in reply. But I sat there, pen in hand, for the longest time without coming up with a single appropriate line, until finally my roommate and I put our heads together and managed to compose a letter. The soldier had to do without a photograph of his intended.

For some reason, the fifteen-and-sixteen-year-old boys from the village seemed to loaf around all day long with nothing to do. With large baskets slung over their shoulders, whenever they saw something that interested them, they picked it up. Sometimes they went out in groups of seven or eight and uprooted young trees alongside the road that were no bigger around than a man's arm. Then they would smack the ground with them and shout loudly—"Ha! Ha! Ha!" as they hunted around for wild rabbits.

Three or four of them came rushing into our vegetable plot one day, clamoring and yelling for all they were worth. They said there was a "cat" in one of the vegetable beds. "Cats" were what they called rabbits. I told them there were no cats here. The rabbit that was hiding among the cabbage leaves knew instinctively that there wasn't enough cover to protect him, so he darted out like a flash. He was much too fast for any of the dogs chasing him, but under the direction of the young hunters, they split up and went after him from different directions. The rabbit changed course several times until he was surrounded by the dogs. He jumped into the air, as high as six or seven Chinese feet, and when he hit the ground he was set upon by the dogs. I felt so frightened and sorry for him when he jumped that my heart nearly broke. From then on, the coarse, loud shouts of "Ha! Ha! Ha!" held no attraction for me to go take a look.

On one occasion—at about three o'clock in the afternoon of January 3rd, 1971—some people came up to me suddenly and, pointing to a couple of grave mounds beyond the vegetable plot to the southeast, asked if that was the cadre-school cemetery. Just after the first contingent of people from the Study Division had arrived in the countryside, one of the tractors had been crossing a bridge when it flipped over into the water and the driver was drowned. The newcomers asked me if that's where the man was buried. I told them no, then pointed off into the distance to where the cemetery was located. A little while later I noticed several men digging a pit on the bank of the stream east of the turnip field. A big cart, the bed of which was covered with a reed mat, was parked alongside them.

Ah! Were they going to bury a corpse? A few men in military uniforms stood off to the side—they were probably from the Propaganda Section.

I watched from a distance as three or four of them dug the pit, their movements extremely rapid. One of them jumped down into the pit to continue the digging. The others soon followed. Then all of a sudden, one of them ran toward me. I assumed that he was thirsty, but he actually wanted to borrow a shovel, for the handle of his had snapped in two. I went into the shed and got one for him.

At the time there wasn't a local villager to be seen anywhere—the only people around were the men digging the pit, busily, urgently. After a while all I could see of them were their heads and shoulders—the pit was deep enough. They pulled back the reed mat and lifted a corpse dressed in a blue uniform out of the cart. I could feel my heart thumping wildly as I watched them bury the body off in the distance.

When the man came back to return the shovel to me, I asked him if the deceased had been a man or a woman, and what the cause of death had been. He told me that they were from a certain company, that the deceased was a suicide, thirty-three years of age, a male.

The winter days were short, and night was beginning to fall by the time they began driving the cart away. Not a soul was left on the now bleak and desolate vegetable plot. I trotted over to the gravesite. It was nothing more than an earthen mound that looked like a huge steamed bun, and no one would ever notice that a new grave had been dug on the bank of the stream.

I related this incident to Mo-cun on the following day

and told him to be careful not to step on the new grave, since they had buried the man without a coffin. When he returned from the post office, where there was plenty of talk about the incident, he had not only learned the name of the deceased, but that he had a wife and children, and that several suitcases were being sent back to his hometown that very day.

One day not long after that there was a heavy snowfall. I was worried that after the snowfall the ground would loosen and the grave cave in until the body was exposed enough for the dogs to get at it. As it turned out, the ground did give way, but not enough to open up the grave.

I kept a solitary watch over the vegetable plot all winter long. In the mornings when the sun made its first appearance, the clouds in half the eastern sky were bathed in radiant colors. From villages far and near, groups of people of all ages wearing brightly colored but tattered clothes emerged one after the other. When they reached the vicinity of the vegetable plot, they broke up into groups of two or three and disappeared in all directions. They drifted back and reformed into groups at sundown, carrying their loads on their backs as they headed home. I bought my dinner and returned to the plot, where I often stood in the doorway of the shed as I slowly ate my meal. The sunsets would grow darker and darker, the evening mist would become heavier. The vast fields were dim as far as the eye could see; not a single person was out there, and there were no lights to be seen. I went back into the shed, where all I could hear were hordes of rats scurrying around in the sorghum stalks—the dry leaves made a loud rustling sound. I ladled out some water to wash my bowl and spoon, then locked the door behind me and headed back to the dormitory.

Everyone was busy with all the work to be done; I alone had time on my hands, and my idleness nagged at me, frustrated me. Although I wasn't a busy "arms instructor of the mighty Imperial Guards," at least I had the sort of feeling that Zu Zhishen must have had when he went up to the monastery on Mt. Wutai to become a monk.[12]

While I was living with one of the local families, since my roommates and I worked at different places, it was inconvenient to join up with them for the walk back to the village. So I made the round trips alone, which gave me a sense of freedom and comfort. Besides, I enjoyed walking down dark roads. If I carried a flashlight, which lit up only a small space wherever I pointed it, I never knew exactly where I was. So by walking down dark roads I got to the point where I knew the surrounding areas well. I walked back to the village along a winding, uneven, rock-strewn path. From the neighboring villages I could occasionally see a flash of light from amidst the trees, but the light I was heading toward was by my bed, that tiny spot of real estate beneath my mosquito net—it was a lonely place to return to, for it wasn't my home. This often reminded me of a painting I had once seen: an old man with a bag slung over his back and a cane in his hand walking step by step down a mountain path directly into his own grave. That's pretty much how I felt about myself.

[12]Another of the heroes in the novel *Shuihu zhuan*, nicknamed The Tattooed Monk, who is not accustomed to a monastic life of inactivity.

After New Year's, on Tomb-Sweeping day (lunar April 5th) to be exact, the Study Division cadre school was moved to a place called Minggang. Before we made the move, our entire unit went to the original vegetable plot, where we dismantled all the structures we had put up. Everything that could be moved or taken apart was. Then the tractors came and levelled the ground. On the eve of our departure, Mo-cun and I slipped over to the plot to take one last look around. The shed was gone, the well platform was gone, the irrigation ditches were gone, the vegetable beds were gone, and even the small mound of earth had disappeared from sight; all that was left was a piece of empty land strewn with clods.

Quickie: A Loving Companion

IV

ONE DAY a poet from our vegetable-plot unit brought a brown puppy over to us from the brick kiln. The poet's name was Ou, a word people occasionally mispronounced Qu. A-xiang jokingly called the puppy "Xiao Qu" (Little Qu), as though naming her after the poet. The poet got back at her very cleverly, not by calling the puppy "Xiao Xiang" (Little Xiang) but by calling her "A-qu," thereby making it sound as if the two were sisters. But "Xiao Qu" (or "Quickie") had a better ring to it than "A-qu," so that's what we called her. Fortunately, no one outside our vegetable-plot detail knew the significance of the name and its relationship to the poet.

We built Quickie a little doghouse alongside the southern wall of the shed, using castoff bricks, and made her a bed out of sorghum stalks. The doghouse was cold and hard, and with the area all around it crisscrossed with irrigation ditches, the first few times the puppy emerged from it she invariably fell into the water. I had stepped into the water once when the weather was still warm, soaking my shoe and sock, which stayed wet all day long and felt terribly uncomfortable. So it pained me to see Quickie covered with water and mud after one of her falls, so cold that she was shivering. If the ground around the shed had been covered with rice stalks, I could have gathered up a handful and wiped her off with them. But the sorghum stalks were too rough to serve my purpose. So all we could do was get her to go out and dry off in the sun. But the sun during those days was at its weakest, and not only was there precious little warmth, but the winds actually chilled the air.

Although Quickie was a puppy from an impoverished out-of-the-way place in the Henan countryside, as long as she was still with her mother there was at least a little milk for nourishment. We had no decent food for her to eat, so we were forced to feed her potato scraps and pieces of steamed buns steeped in water to make them soft, all of which we took from the kitchen. When one of the members of our unit, an old man whose ideology was considered absolutely "correct," saw that we were feeding the dog steamed buns made out of bleached flour (even though it was all discarded scraps), he really read the riot act to our unit leader: "Just you take a look at what our villagers here are eating! And you're feeding a dog food made out of bleached flour!" We all felt such a sense of shame over this that from then on we dared only feed Quickie scraps of potatoes from our own plates. Actually, it didn't make much difference, since neither steamed buns nor potatoes are proper food for dogs. Quickie was, as a result, thin and delicate, and never did grow very big.

One day A-xiang walked over with a bashful look on her face and whispered in my ear: "I've got something to tell you." Then she laughed an embarrassed laugh, finally saying: "Quickie...did you know? She's in the outhouse... eating...excrement!"

I laughed in spite of myself. "The way you look, I thought for a minute it was you who was eating it!"

But A-xiang was worried: "She's getting used to it, so what are we going to do? It's filthy!"

I told her that every dog in the village ate excrement. Shortly after my daughter had arrived in the countryside, a baby who slept on the same earthen *kang* had had a bowel movement right on the bed mat, which my flustered daughter tried to clean up with a handful of toilet paper. One of the village women ran up and rebuked her over wasting not only the toilet paper but the excrement as well. Then she called out, "Wu—lu lu lu lu," after which a dog came rushing in, jumped up onto the *kang*, and began licking at the mess, licking it all clean, including the baby's buttocks. There was no need to wash it off or wipe it clean. So every morning when I heard my neighbors calling their dogs with shouts of "Wu—lu, lu, lu, lu," I knew that their babies were feeding the family dogs.

It took this move to the countryside for me to learn why pigs are such obnoxious animals. The pigs and the dogs were reduced to eating the same stuff, but the pigs lacked the dogs' "manners," they fought for the "food," behaving like "pigs," to the point that they would knock down whoever was squatting in their midst. But the dogs just kept their distance, waiting patiently nearby; then when it was time to move in, they walked over, wagging their tails, and enjoyed their meal. Since we lived in the village, not only did we get to know all the village dogs, but we even shared in their care and feeding.

If pigs and dogs are unclean animals, does that mean that vegetables are unclean plants? Where do the vegetables get their nutrition? Vegetarians probably never give this any thought.

I told A-xiang that we had a couple of sayings for people who are incorrigible or whose true nature will show no matter what. One was: "There's as much chance of your changing as a dog's not eating shit." The other was: "You're just like a dog taking a vow of abstinence before a honey bucket!" Since Quickie wasn't a foreign dog, she had never tasted the canned dogfood made in the West. She wasn't even as well off as the dogs belonging to the other companies, for rumor had it that they had enough kitchen scraps to feed their dogs, which grew plump and had shiny coats. But only pigs, which were considered part of the production process, were allowed to eat our kitchen scraps. Quickie ate whatever she could as a solution to the problem of her own survival.

Whenever Mo-cun came over to the vegetable plot, he brought Quickie scraps of pork skin with the bristles still on it or bones with some of the tendons still attached. So she always jumped up and down in welcome whenever she saw him coming. On one occasion, he brought a couple of spoiled eggs with him that someone had thrown away. He tossed one over to Quickie, who gobbled it down, shell and all. During the time that I was keeping a lone watch over the vegetable plot, Quickie always stuck by me, waiting for Mo-cun. When she spotted him way off in the distance walking toward us from the brick kiln to the north, she ran out to greet him, jumping and barking, and wagging her tail a mile a minute. And as though that weren't enough to express her joy, she would run around him and roll over, get back to her feet and start wagging her tail and jumping again, then fall to the ground and roll over once more. I doubt that Mo-cun had ever been welcomed so enthusiastically in his whole life. It was so overwhelming that the only way he could press forward was for me to shout at Quickie to get out of his way. Then the three of us would walk over to the plot together.

One of my colleagues was constantly telling me about his precious little grandson. According to him, this three-year-old boy always welcomed his granddad home by hopping and jumping like crazy and rolling around on the floor. After telling me this he would laugh and laugh. I've always thought that children are cute, but I stopped short of comparing the man's grandson with Quickie. Yet I often wondered: do dogs have human traits? Or do humans have canine traits? Or is it that when they're still quite young, whether they are babies or puppies, they share universal traits?

When Quickie saw a familiar face, she stuck to the person like glue. Before our company moved to the Central Compound, whenever A-xiang and I walked back to the company area to eat, Quickie followed at our heels. At the time she was only a little puppy, like a baby just learning to walk, and the way she stumbled along awkwardly really endeared her to us. We were concerned that all that walking would tire her out, so we tried to keep her from following us by putting her into the doghouse and blocking up the entrance with a brick. One evening, as we were about half way down the road to the company area, we spotted her sneaking up behind us; she had apparently escaped from the doghouse. It had been raining not long before that, which made the going rough. We yelled at her angrily, but it had no effect on her. She just kept on coming, slipping and sliding on the road as she did, and followed us right into the shed that served as our kitchen and dining hall. The people inside, all of whom loved and pitied her, immediately fed her scraps from their own plates. After she had eaten her fill, she followed our unit leader back to the vegetable plot. This was the first time she had ventured so far from home.

When I first began watching over the vegetable plot by myself, I went over to Mo-cun's to eat my meals, and since the doghouse couldn't hold Quickie, I had to lock her up in the shed. Once, when I had walked all the way past the brick kiln, I looked behind me and spotted her following me stealthily at a distance. She had obviously managed to break out of the shed through one of the sorghum-stalk walls. I called her to a halt, and she froze in her tracks. But when I reached Mo-cun's dormitory, there she was right behind me. As soon as she set eyes on Mo-cun, she started jumping around happily. Mo-cun's roommates fell in love with this little puppy and fought over who was going to feed her first. So once again Quickie ate her fill.

At first Quickie was little more than a welcoming committee of one where Mo-cun's arrivals were concerned, but as time went on, she wouldn't leave his side, although she would only follow him as far as the stream before coming back. One time he spotted her following him after he had walked a long way down the road. Concerned that she would be all tired out, he picked her up and carried her back to the vegetable plot, where he told me to hold onto her before hurrying off himself. To everyone's surprise, after he had returned with the mail, there she was, waiting for him in the doorway of the dormitory, jumping up and down and barking out a welcome. Once she had welcomed him home, she returned to the vegetable plot to keep me company.

After our company moved over to the Central Compound, Quickie survived on leftovers brought back to her from the dining hall by our unit leader, until she was moved over to the Central Compound to be with us for the sake of convenience. There were always some leftovers around the kitchen that she could eat, but this move terminated her contact with the old vegetable plot, and since I didn't return until late at night, at first I didn't even know where her doghouse was. Many of the people in our company were dog lovers, but there were some who felt that dogs were nothing but playthings for the wives and daughters of capitalists. That's why I was always very cool in the way I treated Quickie and avoided showering her with affection. I don't know how she did it, but she very early found out where I was living. Often, when I returned to my room at night, someone would tell me: "That Quickie of yours came looking for you several times today." I was touched by her devotion, but the only way I could reciprocate was to give her things like bones to show how I felt. Later on, she tried to follow me each morning as I set out for the vegetable plot; I invariably shouted her to a halt, and once I even had to throw some dirt clods at her before she'd stop—she just gazed at me from where she was standing. One sprinkly day, as I was sitting alone in the shed, I heard a sudden "ruff!" Quickie came bounding in the door, wagging her tail happily and barking nonstop. Then she came over and sat down next to me. She had found her way from the Central Compound to the vegetable plot all by herself!

If I went over to Mo-cun's to eat, it always took at least half an hour to walk there and back, and since I didn't want to leave the plot unattended for too long, I usually went over to the dining hall at the foot of Tiger Mountain to buy my meals, since it was only a walk of five or six minutes each way. But Quickie was making a guest call on me this time, so I had to treat her to a meal. I normally only bought a half portion of rice and vegetables, but that day I bought a full portion, which I planned to share with Quickie. Granted it was only a short walk back to the plot, but a cold wind blew the whole time, and my hands were unable to shield the bowls of food from the cold wind. The food was ice-cold by the time we got back, and I had to warm it in my mouth before swallowing it. But Quickie wasn't about to wait for me to finish before getting fed herself, so she jumped around begging for her share. I had to hold my ricebowl up as high as I could and alternately eat one spoonful and place another on a piece of paper for her. If I hadn't, she would have forgotten about manners altogether and started licking my bowl and spoon. That was how we shared the pleasure of a meal together, after which I washed the bowl and spoon, got everything together, and took Quickie back to the Central Compound.

Not only was this companion of mine unable to protect me, I found myself actually having to look out for her. For she had, in the space of two or three months, grown from a baby into a young canine lady. There was a ferocious dog named "Tiger" who made his home in a pile of lumber on Tiger Mountain, and another gray dog that was only slightly less ferocious than Tiger. Both of them were clearly attracted to Quickie, who was still small enough to fear them instinctively. So every time she kept me company at the vegetable plot, I had to be her bodyguard on the way home, scaring off the other two dogs. We had to walk alongside a river for a considerable distance; I walked along the crest of the dike, while Quickie very alertly made her way through the surrounding hills, where she could duck out of sight if necessary. She wouldn't put her fears out of her mind until we had crossed the bridge to the other side of the river.

Fortunately, I was very familiar with both of the other dogs; I had, in fact, deliberately gotten friendly with them. One evening I'd taken so long to eat my dinner that by the time I'd locked up the shed, night had already fallen. Just as I started out on the western road I heard barking sounds, but all I could see in front of me was a pair of shiny eyes. Then a big black dog came into view; its back was arched and it was staring at me ferociously—it was Tiger, the meanest dog in the entire Study Division cadre school. Earlier, while I had been living with the local family, if I had somehow missed the road I customarily took back to the village at night, the moment I hesitated, the local dogs would start barking up a storm and rush toward me from all directions. Then I'd have to stand stock-still and, mimicking the tone of voice of my village hosts, yell out: "Dog!"—I'd been told that none of the village dogs had names—before they would slowly back off. This time Tiger came rushing up to me without a sound of warning, throwing a real scare into me. But out of habit I stood stock-still and yelled: "Tiger!" To my surprise, he stopped where he was and just barked and sniffed at my feet, then backed off and started walking away. From then on, whenever I ran across Tiger after buying my meal, I called out his name and gave him something to eat. I've forgotten the gray dog's name, but he and Tiger spent most of their time together. I hailed them whenever I spotted them, for I had never forgotten what I had been taught as a child: you must never show a dog that you are intimidated by it. Evidently I never gave them the impression that I was weak and easily frightened.

After moving to the Central Compound, we took turns making night patrols. Each company had its own procedures; for us the night was divided into four patrols of two hours each. The first patrol was from ten o'clock to midnight, the last one from four to six in the morning. These two patrols were assigned to the sick and elderly for their own good, since it was always better to go to sleep late or wake up early than to have your sleep interrupted in the middle of the night. The patrols were made up of two people, except for the first one, which had only one. This watch was considered safer than the others, since most of the thefts occurred during the early morning hours of three or four o'clock. No one else was particularly eager to go out on patrol alone, but since I preferred to go to bed late, I volunteered for the first watch, and had no competition for the honor. Draping around my shoulders the long and large fur coat that belonged to the company, and carrying a flashlight in my hand, I began my patrol around the dormitory after ten o'clock lights-out. The area of patrol was quite vast: from the road to the north, I had to skirt around the public square where the movies were shown, then pass alongside the new vegetable plot and the pigpens before coming back around to the starting point. Within ten minutes of lights-out, the entire area was silent and there were no other people to be seen—just a lone individual making her rounds, the time passing excruciatingly slowly. But I wasn't always alone: much of the time, Quickie would yelp once or twice, then rush over and keep me company for several of my rounds.

And every time Quickie accompanied me, I was reminded of the cat, Little Flower, who had always greeted me when I returned home each night during the "three-antis" movement[13] at Tsinghua University. I had always been a "scairdy cat": whether there are such things as ghosts or not I can't say, but I was afraid of them nonetheless. And my timidity didn't surface only in the dark, either; I would experience a sudden twinge of cowardice

[13]A 1952 political campaign launched to oppose corruption, waste, and bureaucracy.

even when the darkness around me was broken by the rays of nearby lamps, and it got so bad that I wouldn't even go from one room to another. But I changed completely during the "three-antis" movement, suddenly finding myself unafraid of ghosts. Our nightly department meetings weren't over until eleven or twelve o'clock at night, but I walked alone from the northwest corner of Tsinghua University all the way to my dormitory in the southeast corner of the campus. There were a few spots along the way that had always frightened me before, sometimes so badly that I shivered when I passed them in the daytime when I was alone, or at dusk, even if someone was with me. But during the "three-antis" campaign, I wasn't the least bit afraid. In those days Mo-cun was on a temporary assignment out of town, A-yuan was in school elsewhere in the city and lived in a dormitory, and the housekeeper would already be in bed; that left only Litte Flower, who would wait in a clump of trees about halfway up the road for me to return home. Like Quickie, she would make a soft sound, then dart over beside me, holding lightly onto one of my ankles with her front paws—if I had been as timid as before, this would surely have frightened me out of my wits. After that she'd run ahead a few steps, then come back before turning and running ahead again—back and forth until we were home, where she'd sit in the doorway and wait for me to take out the key and open the door. Quickie was more docile than Little Flower, for she was content to follow closely at my heel. And when she walked along with me, I thought of Little Flower and of things that had happened with her. After we moved away, the cat was lost to us, and we never had the heart to raise another.

If I had borne in mind the Buddhist discipline of "never sleep under a mulberry tree for three consecutive nights," I wouldn't have gotten emotionally involved with a dog that belonged to everyone. But Quickie seemed to have adopted me, or maybe it was just that she sensed I was incapable of abandoning her.

On one occasion, one of the members of our company rode his bike over to a place called Xincai, and Quickie followed him the entire way. That particular comrade was a dog lover, so he bought a bowl of noodles expressly for Quickie, then carried her back home in the basket of his bicycle. This trip so exhausted her that she lay down as soon as she got home and neither twitched a muscle nor made a sound. Everyone thought that she was dying, and when I returned home from the vegetable plot, someone said to me: "I think your Quickie is dying—go take a look!" I ran over there with him, calling out, "Quickie" as soon as I got there. Recognizing my voice, she jumped to her feet and began to bark and wag her tail. Everyone breathed a sigh of relief: "Great," they said, "just great! Quickie's alive!" Quickie couldn't have known that so many people were so concerned over her well-being.

Over New Year's, the kitchen bought a dog to cook and serve, since dogmeat was cheaper than pork. Some of the villagers were dog lovers who couldn't bear to sell theirs, others were willing to part with their dogs but hadn't the heart to slaughter them, while still others were prepared to kill *and* sell theirs. The dog our kitchen bought had already been killed. According to Northerners, in order to cook dogmeat you had to use hardwood for the fire, then cook the meat until it was tender but not overdone, and smother it with garlic sauce. I wonder if Lu Zhishen ate it that way?[14] Following A-xiang's suggestion, our kitchen prepared it with a thick red paste, then added extra onions and ginger and braised it. That night when I returned to the company area for dinner, I made a point of buying a portion of the braised dogmeat to see what it was like; I also let some of the other people have a taste. The meat was extremely tender and not overly lean—pretty much the same as lean pork. Everyone said that Quickie had refused to eat the dogmeat, either raw or cooked. The poet, Mr. Ou, told me that Quickie had held a piece of the meat in her mouth, dug a hole in the ground, and buried it. Not believing him, I asked if he was sure, and he swore that he had seen her do it. But I was convinced that this was nothing more than a figment of a poet's vivid imagination.

Suddenly the news reached us that the cadre school was to move en masse. We were informed by the leadership that all dogs were to be left behind. Just before the move took place, a company of PLA soldiers was quartered in our Central Compound, so A-xiang and I took Quickie over and introduced the soldiers to her, saying that since we couldn't take her with us, we hoped that they would look after her. One of them said: "Don't you worry, we'll be happy to take care of her. A lot of us are pet lovers." A-xiang and I told him that her name was "Quickie,"

[14]Another reference to The Tattooed Monk, who, unable to endure the abstemious life of the monastery, one day gorges himself on dogmeat with garlic sauce, washed down with a bucketful of wine (See Chapter 4 of *Shuihu zhuan*. The author, however, put it as onion sauce.)

which we called out a few times so he would know the sound to which she responded.

Moving day was so chaotic that no one laid eyes on Quickie—most likely she was out playing with one of the other dogs. Once we were settled in Minggang, one of the people returned to the Central Compound to take care of some unfinished business, and when he returned he passed on to us what he had been told there: "That little dog of yours refuses to eat; all she does is run around the place, barking up a storm as though she were looking for something or someone." Was she looking for me? Or Mo-cun? Or any of the people from our company who were so concerned about her? Some of us regretted that we hadn't followed the example of other companies, who had disobeyed the orders and brought their dogs with them to Minggang anyway. But all those dogs were driven away in the end, anyway.

Whenever Mo-cun and I reminisced about Quickie, we generally mused: "I wonder what's become of her?"

Mo-cun's usual answer was: "Maybe she's already been eaten and is now nothing more than a pile of manure."

My answer was: "Well, maybe she has, and maybe she's a mother by now, eating manure to stay alive and having one litter of puppies after another..."

Adventure: While All Ends Well

V

NO ONE assigned to the cadre school in Xi County will ever forget the rain there. It was a gray pall of rain that enveloped the world of man; the ground turned into a muddy quagmire, and even the floors of our rooms were so damp they seemed about to turn to mud. Even though the muddy roads had ruts that were as hard as iron after baking in the hot sun and raised blisters on our feet, the next rainfall turned them into rivers of mud, so slippery and hazardous that even a walking stick was little protection against losing our footing. We were lodged with local families in various villages, and when we walked over to the kitchen to eat our meals, some of us would be all muddy from having slipped and fallen on the road. Our kitchen dining room was nothing more than a mat-shed; alongside it was another shed in which the carts and tools were stored. We would push our way as far inside the sheds as possible, ricebowls in hand, since the floor in the middle was comparatively dry. The farther from the center we stood, the muddier the flooring and the greater the risk of getting soaked by the rain that blew inside. But whether we were in the middle of the sheds or near the edges, there was no place to hide from the water that dripped from the roofs. When the meal was over, we had to slip and slide through the mud over to the well where we washed our ricebowls. Then on the road back to the villages we had to be especially careful not to drop and break our thermos bottles; that would have been an irreversible disaster, since thermos bottles were not available locally, nor could we have had them sent from Peking. Ai! The rain in Xi County was totally debilitating.

One afternoon, during a rainstorm that had lasted several days, we held a study-session meeting in the village; after lunch, only the core or key members of the leadership met, leaving the rest of us free to do whatever we pleased. Many of us returned to the homes of our villagers to write letters, mend clothing, or make winter clothes. I was living in the home of the vice-commander of a unit at the time, and although his home was constructed of mud-packed walls, ceiling, and floor, it was better maintained than most; the wall facing south even had a window, a hole a foot wide and a half foot in height. We covered the window with a layer of paper, which kept out the wind but let in some light. My bed was in a corner of the room that was protected from the wind, but it was so dark there that I couldn't see my fingers when I held them in front of my face. So other than as a place to sleep at night, it didn't hold the slightest attraction for me. The only light in the entire room was provided by the weak rays that filtered in through the window, and I had no desire to make any use of it. Besides, it was too much work to have to keep changing out of the battle gear that protected me from the rain—raincoat, rainpants, rainboots—which was forever coated with mud. I kept my dripping umbrella nearby, and all I had to do was pick it up with one hand and my walking stick with the other and head out into the rain.

One of the things I loved most about my hometown of Suzhou (Soochow) was the rain. The leaves on the trees in our rear garden turned the color of jade when they were washed clean of all their dust. I felt that my body was refreshed, my heart cleansed. But the rain in Xi County made a person feel as though she were made of clay, that even her bones had congealed into a mass of gooey mud. I walked out of the village atop a sea of mud. I looked at my watch—it was only a little past two o'clock—and I felt a sudden desire to go see Mo-cun. I knew that it was against regulations to go see him without first getting permission, but at that time they wouldn't blow the bugle, line us up in formation, or take roll. I decided to sneak around the kitchen and take the western road.

The fields around me were all laid out with irrigation ditches; normally dry, they turned into rivers of water following the rains. As I crossed a small bridge I was faced with a pathway that was completely flooded, the water mixing with that in the irrigation ditches to form a small river. But it was only a matter of a few steps before I could be on the road itself, and since I wasn't about to turn back then, I very gingerly stepped into the shallow water on the bank. There were a few spots on the uneven ground where the water was relatively deep, but I somehow managed to cross to the crest of the bank without incident. Taking a look behind me, I was relieved to find that I was not being pursued, so I stepped onto the road and headed west, making a mental note to take a different route on my return trip.

The mud on the road forced me to go slowly, one cautious step at a time. My rainboots grew heavier with each step, so that every so often I had to stop and scrape off the mud with my walking stick. I was wearing high-topped rainboots, but the sticky mud along the way soon clung to them and weighted them down so heavily that it was as though eunuchs were vying to relieve me of my boots.[15] More than once I nearly walked right out of my boots when they stuck in the mud. Not only that, several mud clods somehow worked their way into the boots themselves. Although I started out walking on the southern edge of the road, there seemed to be more twigs and grass on the northern edge, which would have made for surer footing, so I moved over there. But then it seemed to me that there was more grass on the southern edge. It was a wide road, level and straight for all but the last twenty or thirty feet before the brick kiln, where it was all caved in. Back when

[15]The author has made a pun here; the eunuch allusion refers to the Tang dynasty eunuch Gao Lishi, the favorite of the emperor Ming Huang (712-755).

we had begun digging the well for our vegetable plot, and A-xiang and I had been responsible for bringing the workers their meals, it was she who had taken control of the cart at this spot, pushing it up and over the bumps. Since it had rained for several days, this spot had now turned into a swamp, looking for all the world like a shallow pond, with two embankments running right down the middle. I stepped up onto one of the embankments and promptly sank into the water; it had only been a ridge formed by passing carts, and once it was saturated with water it crumbled as soon as it was touched. I'd trudged this far, which hadn't been easy even if it was a broad, flat road, and I wasn't about to turn back then, even though the water only lacked a couple of inches of completely covering my rainboots. Some of the ground beneath the water was sandy, while in other spots it was grassy; both the sandy and grassy spots were sometimes spongy, sometimes firm. I pressed on, one tentative step after another, using my walking stick for added support, until, to my own amazement, I forded the pond without incident.

Once I had reached the brick kiln at the top of the little hill, I had to turn and head north. A small river running from north to south flowed to the foot of the hill on which the brick kiln stood; the slightest rise in the water level carried the river into the lower marshes of the wasteland to the west. Normally the river meandered past that spot at the foot of the hill, but after a heavy rainfall, the water rose until the spot became an island in the midst of rapidly flowing water. I walked along the northern bank, watching the expanse of water grow broader and broader. Mo-cun's dormitory was located on the other side, where he lived in the last of several rows of gray, tiled buildings. By the time his dormitory was in sight, the river was at least three meters across. A small bridge that was no more than four or five feet in length had been washed away and was now floating in a heap downstream. In the torrential downpour, the sky and the ground seemed to have fused together. But the three-meter-wide river in front of me had cut the road off completely. From where I stood on the eastern bank, I gazed across to the western bank at Mocun's dormitory, which was the westernmost of the more than ten buildings in this particular row. I looked and looked, without spotting a single person, and just then I realized what a laughingstock I'd be if anyone saw me standing there. So all I could do was turn and make my way back down the muddy road. I planned my course back as I walked along: the farther south I went, the narrower the river became and the faster the water flowed. Now if I went all the way to the foot of the hill beneath the brick kiln and hopped over into the little island, then jumped across to the other side, wouldn't that put me where I wanted to be? As I looked over at the other side I saw nothing but rock-strewn ground, with no road in sight; but at least over there I could count on an open stretch of ground, unbroken by any river. However, the footing was very slippery on the riverbank, and I couldn't be as sure of my footing in rainboots as I would in cloth shoes. Another question mark had to do with the firmness of the mud on the little island. I tested the ground with my walking stick, and it seemed firm enough, so I stuck the end of the walking stick deeply in the ground and vaulted over onto the island, then repeated the procedure to jump over to the opposite bank. The road back was full of bumps and hollows, and if I wasn't stepping into mud I was sloshing through water; but after more hardships and obstacles than I could count, I somehow managed to make it to the front door of Mo-cun's dormitory.

I opened the door and walked in, much to his surprise. "What are you doing here?"

"I came to see you," I said with a smile.

He really gave me a piece of his mind and insisted that I return home. I was well aware that I couldn't stay there long, for a glance at my watch showed that it had taken me more than double the time it normally took to make the trip. I also had a nagging fear that the little island would continue to shrink in size, until I could no longer cross the river. And if the already leaden sky turned any darker, I'd be sure to trip and fall in the mud as I made my way across the pond.

As luck would have it, one of the men had some business to take care of at the Central Compound and would be passing right by the brick kiln as he headed west. I told him that the bridge was washed out, but he said that didn't matter, since there was another route to the south. So I decided to go along with him. Mo-cun put on his rain-boots, took up his umbrella, and walked part of the way with us, before heading back. When we reached the kiln, my companion headed west, while I turned and headed east. Fortunately, this was the same road I had taken just a while earlier, so all I had to do was exercise some patience and caution and I could be a bit bolder. Night had fallen by the time I arrived at our kitchen. It was past dinner time, but a light was still burning inside the shed, and I could hear voices. Just like a thief in the night, I slipped past the kitchen and made my way back to my room as fast as the muddy footing would allow.

I've long since forgotten what I had for dinner that night, whether I had saved half a steamed bun or Mo-cun had given me something to eat; for all I know, I might have gone hungry. I thought only of my good fortune in not having fallen into the river or mud, in having kept my footing, and in having avoided being caught by the leadership; not even my roommates were aware that I had just done a very unusual thing.

As winter arrived, the entire company moved into the buildings we had constructed. The Propaganda Teams wanted us to enjoy a memorable New Year's, so we were treated to a New Year's Eve banquet to keep us from feeling homesick.

The Institute of Foreign Literature had originally been an offshoot of the Institute of Literature. The "old men" of several of the female comrades in my unit (Mo-cun was my "old man"—a woman's husband was referred to as her "old man," regardless of his age) were in the same unit, so we agreed to invite them over to share our New Year's dinner. Each of the cooks in our kitchen prepared his specialty, so we had a great many dishes that night: smoked fish, pickled chicken, braised pork, beef curry, and just about everything else you might expect, including cold vegetables in special sauces; everything was just delicious. Mo-cun spiritedly joined our vegetable-plot detail as we sat around a rectangular table and had a sumptuous spread. Quickie stayed under the table, where she ate her fill, and I wouldn't be surprised if she wagged her tail so hard that night it drooped.

I thought back to when we had celebrated Mo-cun's six-tieth birthday (we had also celebrated my sixtieth birth-day, by Chinese reckoning) by eating only some canned braised chicken. That had been a day off for me, but not for him—a day off meant two meals, a day on meant three. I had gone over to his place that day right after breakfast and had no appetite at noon; then when dinner-time rolled around, I was in such a hurry to get back to my own company that all I had time for was a few bites of a steamed bun. But for this New Year's Eve meal we had good food *and* good wine. Neither of us was a drinker, but we joined the others in enjoying ourselves and putting our cares aside. Then after dinner we headed back toward Mo-cun's place together, chatting about this and that as we walked. When we reached the bridge where the tractor had tumbled into the river, Mo-cun said to me: "You go on back now." Then he crossed the bridge and headed north; he was only halfway home.

That was a day that had followed a heavy snowfall, and the snow on the road had already melted, leaving behind a road caked with mud that was already beginning to harden, even though it was still soft enough to walk on without slipping. But there was still unmelted snow on the narrow road north of the bridge. Night had fallen by then, and I was concerned that Mo-cun, with his myopia, would find it hard to see where he was going—he'd never been much good at finding his way—so I decided to walk him all the way back to his dormitory.

When snow covered the ground, the roads were nearly indistinguishable from the surrounding fields. So I made my way very carefully, fixing each landmark securely in my mind: for instance, how many tall trees there were at a particular bend in the road, how many short trees, the shapes of the branches; a spot where the road veered off to one direction or another; a place where the snow was thicker than at other places, which meant that there was an irrigation ditch beneath my feet, the base of which was partly melted mud, and that I should avoid that spot on my return trip home.

By the time we reached our destination, Mo-cun's room was already flooded with lamplight. I knew I couldn't stay, since it was getting late, so I turned to go. A young man standing nearby offered to walk me home, since it was so dark out, but I thought it would be too great an imposition to make him leave the cozy warmth of his room and the light-hearted conversation of this New Year's Eve just to walk me home on such a dark, cold night. So I politely refused his offer, saying that I knew the way back. But all of this talk had left Mo-cun feeling anxious, so I said boastfully: "I've traveled that road twice a day for as long as I can remember! Besides, I've got a strong flashlight with me, so there's nothing to be afraid of!" Actually, the only roads I used on my daily walks were the dike on the northern side and the wide east-west road paralleling the southern dike. Mo-cun was unaware that in the space of half an hour the sky outside had changed completely and the road was no longer the road we had taken together on our way over. On top of that, finding our way over had been made easier by the lamplight coming from the buildings in front of us; heading the other way into the darkness with the light behind me would be a different matter altogether. But I stood firm in not wanting the man to see me home, and he didn't force the issue. So he walked with me as far as the lamplight reached, where I stopped and sent him back.

I had walked down enough dark roads to feel pretty confident, so I just stood there orienting myself to my surroundings, something that some people said we female comrades were not very good at. I recall reading in a book somewhere that women were like mother hens—they lost their bearings as soon as they left the nest. This may have been an intentional insult to women, but I am definitely one of those creatures who has no sense of direction, who invariably "strikes out for south city only to wind up in north city."[16] Even with Mo-cun's inability to find his way from one place to another, I nonetheless relied upon his sense of direction. But this time I took pains to map out my course: first I'd head southwest and cut across the woods until I reached the wide road running alongside it; then I'd turn to the west until I reached the small cluster of trees; from there I'd turn south, cross the bridge, and walk down that familiar road all the way to my dormitory.

As soon as I was beyond the range of the light from the lamps, I was enshrouded by total darkness. It was a starless night and the ground was blanketed by snow. I could neither see any trees nor find the road. When I turned on my flashlight, all I could see were the tree trunks, some off in the distance, some nearby. I paused to let my eyes get used to the dark, then took a careful look around; but there was nothing to be seen in the pervading darkness except the white snow on the ground. I could no longer even

---

[16]The final line of Du Fu's "Lament By the River's Edge."

catch a glimpse of the little path that wound through the trees, the one that had been vaguely distinguishable at dusk because of the lamplight from the dormitory. I felt the urge to turn back and ask the young man to see me home after all, but I quickly realized that even a second pair of eyes wouldn't make it any easier to find the road with all this snow on the ground. Besides, if he did see me home, he'd have to make the return trip all by himself, so it was still up to me to forge ahead as best I could.

I knew that the ground beneath my feet wasn't going to move on its own while I stood there trying to make up my mind, so I braced myself and headed into the darkness in a roughly south-eastern direction. If I were to go a little too far to the west, I'd never find my way out of the woods, so I chose to take a more southerly route. I could see the layer of snow beneath my feet, but each footstep left a muddy imprint. Luckily for me, there were enough sorghum stalks, dried grasses, and fallen leaves to keep the footing from getting too slippery. I carefully made my way south, turning to the west whenever my passage was blocked by a tree.

I looked back to see if the lights from Mo-cun's dormitory were still visible—they weren't—and I wasn't sure just where I was at the moment. I continued walking ahead, when suddenly my foot stepped into space and I tumbled into a ditch, scaring myself half to death. But then I recalled that there was a wide, very deep ditch that ran alongside the road next to the woods, and I actually rejoiced over my good fortune in having fallen into it. I quickly turned on my flashlight, found a way out, and climbed up onto the road beside the woods.

Since there was no snow on this road, walking along it was no problem, so I started taking longer strides. But I had to be prepared to turn south at the right place, for if I kept walking straight ahead, I'd wind up at a neighboring village west of the Central Compound. Trees had been planted alongside the road, one every dozen steps or so, but I could only see the trunks, not the branches, the leaves, or the unique shapes of the trees themselves. None of the landmarks I had noted on my way over came into view. I was anxious that I might miss the turnoff and be unable to find the bridge from which the tractor had fallen. If I had to miss it, I'd be better off turning too soon than turning too late, for if I passed the point, I'd drift off into the fields, where I could easily spend the entire night walking around in circles. So the moment I spotted a cluster of trees nearby, I turned abruptly to the south.

As soon as I felt the road my sense of direction deserted me; after a few steps I discovered that I was standing in a clump of sorghum stalks. But I kept walking straight ahead, for as long as I was headed south, sooner or later I'd reach the river, and once I'd done that, I'd be able to find the bridge.

I had once heard someone say that there were bad people who hid themselves in the sorghum fields on dark nights; I was also afraid that wild dogs could hear me coming, so I kept my ears pricked, listening very carefully to the sounds around me as I walked along gingerly, trying to avoid stepping on the dried leaves from the sorghum stalks on the ground around me. The soil was very muddy, but not all that slippery. I relied upon all my senses, preferring not to use my flashlight. I don't know how long I had been walking when I suddenly spotted a road in front of me running from left to right, beyond which rose a tall dike. I'd made it to the river! The only problem was that, with the snow-covered ground and the darkness of the night, that familiar old road had become a stranger, and I didn't know if I was east of the bridge or west of it—for there was a tall dike on the western bank as well. Now if I had already made it to the west bank, the river should widen the farther west it flowed, and I would have to walk all the way to another brick kiln west of the Central Compound before I could cross to the other bank, then turn and head south until I made my way back to my dormitory. I had heard that one of the cadre-school "students" had hanged himself in that kiln recently. Fortunately, I was no longer the "scairdy cat" of former days, for if I had been, just thinking about one man drowning under this very bridge and another hanging himself in the kiln would have been enough to paralyze me with fear right there at the riverside. I suspected that in my impatience I had turned too early and was still on the eastern side of the bridge; so I headed west, and after walking for a while my suspicions were confirmed, for I finally reached the bridge.

Even after crossing the bridge, I still had half the distance to go, so I walked as fast as I could, and before long, I was home.

"Back already?" one of my roommates greeted me with a smile on her face, as though I had just gone out for a little stroll. There in my brightly lit room I could scarcely believe that there was an entirely different world out in the pitch-black wilds.

In the early spring of 1971, the Study Division cadre

school moved en masse from Xi County to a barracks at the Minggang Division Headquarters. The mission for our cadre school was changed from performing labor to "study sessions"—the study of class struggle, we supposed. For those people who hadn't quite comprehended the significance of the abbreviation "Study Division," it now suddenly dawned on them. Of course, "Study Division" was meant to be short for "Study Session Division."[17]

Watching movies must have been considered a study session of sorts, and it sure beat classwork. No one was excused from these sessions (Mo-cun's vision was so poor that he couldn't see what was on the screen, so he was given special dispensation). On nights when movies were shown, right after dinner we all took folding stools and lined up in the public square. Every unit had its own designated area, where each of us sat in close file on our stools. The ground in our particular designated space turned into a quagmire after a rainfall, and we had to set up our stools right there in the mud—sometimes it started raining while we were out there, so we had to take raingear along with us. And during hot nights we were exposed to hordes of mosquitoes. But this sort of class required no examinations. As long as I could keep my eyes open I watched the screen, and when I couldn't I rested. There weren't more than a few movies altogether, so whatever I missed when I rested my eyes I'd have plenty of chances to see later on. After we returned to our dormitory, the thirty women who shared one room would discuss the movie we had just seen, while I would just sit quietly by so as not to show my ignorance on the subject.

[17]See the opening line on page 5.

One night as we were returning to the dormitory after watching a movie, I continued my woolgathering, fixing my gaze on the feet of the person ahead of me as I walked along. I suddenly realized that the ranks ahead were starting to thin, and I soon found myself in the dormitory passageway—but it wasn't *my* dormitory. I quickly disengaged myself from the ranks, of which only the tail-end now remained. Then they too entered the dormitory one by one. I had no idea where my own dormitory was, nor did any of the people I asked. They were too busy returning to their own rooms to pay any attention to me. I suddenly felt like someone who had drifted into a strange town, where she didn't know a soul.

I looked up at the star-filled sky. I knew some of the constellations, but now they all seemed to be out of place. I never did know how to tell directions by the stars, but at least I could see by their placement that I was a long way from my dormitory. The camp occupied a huge area and was comprised of a great many barracks buildings scattered all over the place, all of which were now brightly lit up. I don't know how many roads crisscrossed the camp, but there were plenty. And since every building looked exactly like all the others, if I just started running up one path and down another, once people started turning out their lamps, I wouldn't have a prayer of finding my dormitory. My only chance was to locate the stone-paved road on the southern boundary of the camp, since I could find my way home from there. I knew that the public square where the movies were shown wasn't far from the road, and I suspected that the unfamiliar dormitory I had stumbled upon couldn't be far from the square. Most of the barracks buildings faced south, which meant that the Big Dipper was behind them—I knew that much, at least. So all I had to do was turn my back to this dormitory and I'd be facing south; that should take me up to the road, and even if that turned out to be the long way around, at least the road made for easy walking.

Not wanting to waste any more time, I concentrated on walking due south, instead of following the winding paths, taking whatever shortcuts were necessary, even when it meant cutting across the camp's vegetable plot. This plot was vastly different from ours in Xi County: the soil here was so fertile that the neatly laid out beds were teeming with all kinds of vegetables. I knew that there was one deep manure pit for every one or two vegetable beds, for not long before this, a tall young man in our unit had fallen into one of these pits on the way back from watching a movie. After climbing out, he had gone immediately to the "water house"—which is what we called our shower area—without a thought for how cold it was, and scrubbed himself for the longest time before returning quietly to his room. In this way he managed to avoid making a public spectacle of himself. If I were to fall into one of the pits now, I'd sink straight to the bottom, and none of my shouts would bring anyone to my rescue. As for the terror of taking a shower in ice-cold water, that was an eventuality that didn't even have to be considered.

Since I was always walking in rank, there had been no need to carry a flashlight, so I hadn't paid any attention to the condition of the batteries. Now the flashlight was nearly dead, and all I could see was the leaf-covered ground, although I couldn't tell what kind of vegetables I was walking through. My only protection against falling into one of the pits was something I had learned from Zhu Bajie and his experience with walking across a frozen lake.[18] Now although I didn't have a carrying pole to lay across my shoulder, as he had, I at least had my stool, which I could carry in front of me as an extension of my body. But if I were to fall in up to my waist and my shouts brought no one to my aid, I'd still wind up at the bottom of the manure pit. I forced myself to stop thinking these wild thoughts and concentrated on moving ahead, the stool in one hand, the flashlight in the other. I walked very gingerly, brushing aside vegetable leaves with each step, and although I was feeling pretty anxious, I proceeded with great caution, as though I were on the edge of a deep abyss. I didn't dare make a single false step. I finally crossed the vegetable plot, with considerable difficulty, but as soon as I stepped over an irrigation ditch, I found myself in yet another vegetable plot. It was like a nightmare—I kept walking and walking, but I didn't think I'd ever find my way out of the vegetable plots.

Fortunately I had been heading in the right direction, and at last I emerged from the vegetable plot. I crossed a little asphalt road, a vacant grassy area, and a stone pile, finally setting foot on the paved road I had been looking for. I really started to move then, alternately running and walking fast; before long I was headed west, and from there it was a straight shot back to the dormitory. The lights were still on in the room, and the last group of

[18]Zhu Bajie (Chu Pa-chieh) is one of the main characters in the classical novel *Journey to the West (Xiyou ji)*, translated by Anthony C. Yu (known as Pigsy in Arthur Waley's *Monkey*).

women was just then returning from the toilet. Obviously, I hadn't been out in the fields for even twenty minutes. Luckily I hadn't taken a wrong turn somewhere; it was almost as though I had just returned to the room from a visit to the toilet, and no one would have dreamed that I had followed the wrong group of people with my eyes wide open. I began to wonder when I might have been discovered if I had fallen into one of the manure pits.

I lay down on my hard, sturdy little bed and slept more peacefully that night than any other in memory.

One of my colleagues, who was two years younger than I, was sitting quietly on his stool watching the movie after dinner one night, and suffered a stroke; he was immediately paralyzed and beyond help before we knew it. From then on, the older folks were excused from the movie sessions. I often wondered whether, if I had been forced to shout for help in front of that unfamiliar dormitory, the old folks might have been excused from these sessions even earlier. But then my shouts of distress might not have been tragic enough, and could have been used as a lesson by negative example.

These three incidents were, for me, somewhat dangerous adventures, although, in truth, there wasn't all that much danger involved; they would have been truly dangerous only if they had ended in tragedy.

Wronged: But Home—At Last

VI

WHEN I WAS being put up in Yang Village, the cat belonging to my landlord once played a prank on me. We lit a kerosene lamp in the room each night, which we hung on the wall alongside the door, and since my bed was the farthest from the door, I was always in the shadows. One evening, after my roommate and I had finished washing up at the well, we returned to our room, where I could discern two strange objects on my bed. Fortunately for me, I refrained from reaching out and touching whatever they were; instead I shone my flashlight on the objects, which turned out to be a gutted and bloody dead rat, with its pink innards lying in a heap alongside it. Neither of us had the nerve to pick the things up in our fingers, so I very gingerly removed my comforter and pillow, then my roommate and I lifted up the bedsheet by its corners and carried the dead rat outside, where we dumped it into the compost pit behind the house. I rose early the next morning and washed my bedsheet, using one bucketful of water after another. After washing it several times, I hung it out to dry, then washed it again, and still I thought the bloodstains would never come out.

The next time I saw Mo-cun, I related this ill-omened incident to him, telling him that the cat had "dined" me with a decayed rat. "That's a good omen," he said to console me. "It could mean that you'll be taking leave of this place soon. Having the rat and its innards separated into two piles means 'taking leave of,' while the word 'rat' (*shu*) is roughly homophonous with 'place' (*chu*). I had quite a laugh over the way he so cleverly used dream analysis or word dissection to explain what had happened, even though he must have known that I wasn't about to believe this story he had concocted to make me feel better. I could have responded to him in the manner of the *dazibao* [big-character posters] by shouting: "Your ideological foundation is crystal clear! So you're thinking about leaving this place, huh? Well, you can forget about that!" The truth of the matter was, we both knew that "freedom is the appreciation of necessity": if you know that a door is securely locked, pushing on it or trying to break it down is an exercise in futility.

On one of the last days of the year, during one of our meetings at the vegetable plot, Mo-cun let me in on a very unexpected piece of news.

On his trips to the post office he often helped one of the workers there decipher some of the hard-to-read Chinese characters. He provided a valuable service by locating some of the obscure place names, and the man came to regard him highly, rewarding him for his efforts with glasses of tea. The locals called boiled water "tea," but it was the real stuff that Mo-cun was treated to. It was this comrade who told Mo-cun that a telegram had been received from Peking, which ordered the Study Division cadre school to send a group of its "old, weak, sick, and disabled" members back to the capital, and Mo-cun's name was supposed to be on the list.

I couldn't have been happier, since if Mo-cun could return to Peking, he and A-yuan could rely upon one another to get by. That way I could stay behind alone at the cadre school without any worries; besides, I could make an annual trip back to Peking to visit my family. At the time, no working couples at the Xi County cadre school enjoyed that privilege, even if they weren't actually living together.

A few days later, on one of his return trips from the post office with his sack of mail, he broke precedent by crossing the river to come over and see me; he was making a special trip to pass on the news that the list of approved names of the "old, weak, sick, and disabled" who were to be sent back to Peking had arrived, and his name was on it.

I had already begun thinking about packing for him, and now I could only wait on pins and needles until the date was announced. A few days later, when he came by to see me, his face was as calm as ever.

"Hasn't it been officially announced yet?"

It had, and his name wasn't on it.

As he told me the names of those who were returning to Peking, my heart sank. Had there not been the erroneous information in the first place, there would have been nothing to give rise to hope. Nor would there have been the bitter disappointment that came with frustrated hope.

I accompanied him as far as the riverbank, then walked back to the shed and watched his back as it receded into the distance, a hundred thoughts running through my mind.

Did Mo-cun have more "youthful vigor" than the others? I recited Han Yu's poem "Written For Zhang Gongcao on the Night of August Fifteenth,"[19] and was almost carried away by my emotions.

As I began to recite the poem, I thought of the damning material in Mo-cun's dossier. If it hadn't been for the "Great Proletarian Cultural Revolution" we would never have known about this material.

During the early stages of the "Cultural Revolution," several people had joined forces to put up a *dazibao* denouncing Mo-cun for being contemptuous of the published works of the leader [Mao Zedong]. People who knew Mo-cun, however slightly, reacted to seeing this by saying that if this fellow Qian had said something to that effect, he would certainly have done so in a more witty fashion, and that even the tone wasn't quite right. Someone tipped me off about the *dazibao*, which I went to see. I was

[19]The author implies here that her husband's release from the cadre school was thwarted by someone above him for reasons not made clear here.

furious. I said that in order to "chase the wind and clutch at shadows"—to make groundless accusations—one at least needed some wind and some shadows; people shouldn't be allowed to frame someone without any cause at all. After the two of us had been released from our respective "cowsheds," I told Mo-cun all about the incident. Together we drafted a small-character poster [xiaozibao], spelling out every aspect of the case and demanding a fair investigation. After eating our dinner as fast as we could, we went over to the Study Division with a jar of paste and a flashlight, where we pasted up our xiaozibao directly beneath the dazibao. The next day I was subjected to a no-nonsense struggle session. Some time after this incident I discovered that the accusations in the dazibao hadn't been completely without basis. Someone had in fact accused "this fellow Qian" of saying something along the lines described. Obviously, the accusation had been placed in his dossier without anyone checking to see if it was accurate, and when they did get around to investigating, the "accuser" denied making the accusation. I'm sure that the Red Guards' investigation was a thorough one, but they were unable to produce any proof. Before Mo-cun was sent down to the cadre school, the Propaganda Team considered this "accusation" to be a very serious matter, for even though no proof had surfaced, they were convinced that where there's smoke there's fire, and they ordered him to write a self-examination. He had to handle this tactfully, so he wrote a self-examination that skirted the issues. I still feel a sense of injustice every time I recall this incident.

This time, when Mo-cun came to see me in the vegetable plot, I said to him: "That damning material has come back to haunt you for sure." But he thought I was being silly; since everything had been decided, why worry about what was coming back to haunt him. I admitted that I was being silly, and that it was foolish to engage in wishful thinking; still, what had happened so long ago remained in my heart and wouldn't go away.

On the day the people departed for Peking, we got up early and hurried over to the public square by the highway to give them a sendoff. The feelings that a visitor away from home has when he sees someone off to where he himself came from are quite unique. I felt terribly disappointed as I watched one truck after another pull out with the people and their belongings; just then, one of my female companions took me by the arm and said: "Come on! Let's go back!" So I went with her back to the dormitory, where she sighed long and hard, as though she wanted to say something. But the words wouldn't come, so we retired to our rooms.

Only the "old, weak, sick, and disabled" had returned to Peking, and after we saw them off, we were left with the feeling that we might spend the rest of our lives here at the cadre school. I walked alone over to the vegetable plot, when a new thought suddenly hit me: If I had seen Mo-cun off, could I still experience the sense of "we?" Even though I would still be physically at the cadre school, my mood would be quite different, for I would no longer be able to consider myself a part of "we." I thought back to the days just before Liberation, when so many people had been fleeing the country in alarm; with so many roads open to the two of us, why hadn't we chosen to leave? Had we been progressive thinkers then? Had we had high political consciousness? Mo-cun had often quoted the lines of the poet Liu Yong:

Although my girdle grows loose, I care not;
For her I pine with no regrets.[20]

We had simply been unwilling to abandon the motherland, to cast off the "you;" in other words, it was all tied up with the concept of "we" or "us." And even though we had never met the billion other people who made up this "we," this "us," we were still part of the same body—we all shared a common lot and were closely bound up with one another. We were all indispensable parts of a whole. I was ashamed of myself for having listened to rumors and let myself get carried away with wild thoughts; I had hoped only that Mo-cun could return to Peking and be together with A-yuan again—I couldn't see beyond the well-being of my own family. Since Liberation, after having been through the fire and crucible of reform, I'm afraid that I was worse off than at the very beginning.

Mo-cun walked across the vegetable plot toward me; I pointed to the shed and said: "If they'd give us a shed like that, we could live there together. What do you think?"

He thought it over for a moment, then said: "There aren't any books."

He was right—we could get by without all the other material comforts, but the days would be far too long without any books. All he had in his trunk were things like dictionaries, notebooks, and calligraphy models.

[20]The final two lines of Liu's *ci* (詞) to the tune of *Feng Qi Wu.* Here the "her" clearly refers to the motherland.

"Are you sorry we stayed on back then instead of leaving?" I asked him.

"If I could turn back the clock, I'd probably do the same thing all over again."

Mo-cun had always been one to make up his mind quickly, seemingly without thinking things out first. But once his decision had been made, he stuck by it. I'm the type who tries to think things out from every angle, but we invariably arrive at the same conclusions. Since we had made our decision, and had done so with our eyes open, we stuck to our guns and avoided letting our thoughts get out of hand.

After the cadre school had moved to Minggang, Mo-cun's and my dormitories were separated only by a single row of buildings, so it took no more than five or six minutes to get from one to the other. We lived in large tile-roofed buildings with glass windows and cement floors. The food there was better than it had been at the Study Division dining hall, and we no longer had to put up with toilets with rush walls and shallow pits, nor did we have to stand in line to use them. Our living quarters were spacious enough that we could take our reference books and notebooks out of our trunk and put them to use. Then in addition to a continuous stream of foodstuffs, A-yuan also sent us foreign magazines and newspapers of every type from Peking. And the various books that were circulated secretly among our companions were always worth another reading. Our surroundings were peaceful and beautiful, and there was plenty of room to walk around. The two of us went for a stroll every day at dusk, which was a great improvement over having to meet in the vegetable plot. But since we weren't engaged in either physical or mental labor, we felt ashamed that we weren't earning our keep, and the sight of all those promising young people doing nothing but holding daily meetings and making speeches filled us with secret anxieties.

Absolutely nothing was done at the cadre school, but still we couldn't leave. Even though no more than an hour's walk separated us from the train station, without written authorization from the Propaganda Team, no one could buy a ticket. Once when Mo-cun had a toothache and I had an eye infection, we chose a date to request permission to see a doctor at Xinyang. The hospital there had developed a new technique called massage extraction— they'd massage the gums, then extract the teeth. But there were no volunteer patients, for everyone ran away from the treatment. Mo-cun and I went out and took a stroll through one of the area's scenic spots, the name of which escapes me now. The "mountain" was an earthen mound, the "lake" a nearly dried-up pond; there was a dilapidated bridge and several patches of medicinal plants growing in the "valleys." Even though there wasn't much to do there, our spirits were extremely high, because we had been given a day off from our studies. After that I went by myself to Xinyang to have my eye checked, and discovered that my tear duct was torn. I was advised to go to Peking to have it taken care of, but the Propaganda Team would not permit it under any circumstances. So I requested a leave of absence to return to Peking, for which I had to get authorization from the Study Division before I would be allowed to register at the hospital. This rule was probably instituted to keep the people at the cadre school from going to Peking on the pretext of seeking a doctor, then not returning.

Anyone who came down with a major illness at the cadre school was completely at the mercy of Lady Luck. On my return from Peking, after having had my eye taken care of, I brought A-yuan back with me on a family visit. We presumed that Mo-cun would be there to meet us when we arrived in Minggang, but when we got off the train, we didn't spot him anywhere on the platform. We continued looking for him outside the station and on the road all the way back to the cadre school, afraid that we had missed him at the train station and that he was still there looking for us. Who could have guessed that after I had left for Peking, he would have taken seriously ill with asthma and a high fever! A-yuan and I weren't informed of this until we were almost at his dormitory. The medical worker assigned to his company wouldn't even qualify as a "bare-foot doctor." She herself told me that this was the first time in her life she had ever given an intravenous injection, and she had been so nervous that she had broken out in a sweat; then after injecting the needle she had even forgotten to remove the rubber tourniquet she had wound around Mo-cun's upper arm. But after two injections, his condition improved, and by the time A-yuan and I arrived at the cadre school, his temperature had already subsided. The medical worker kept pointing to herself, throwing her head back, and saying: "Mr. Qian, you know I saved your life!" Indeed it was fortunate she had been around. If she had been afraid or unwilling to give those two injections and Mo-cun had been sent somewhere far away for treatment, things could have turned out much worse.

A-yuan's family visit lessened our concerns about one another slightly. However, eating three square meals a day without doing any work caused us some anxiety. Following newspaper reports that Lin Biao had "kicked the bucket," the struggle against May Sixteenth elements lost its momentum. But all of the "old, weak, sick, and disabled," who had returned to Peking still did nothing but attend meetings and study sessions.

It has been said that if you hope for something long enough, your hope will someday be realized, but by the time it is, it will have undergone a change. In March, 1972, a second group of "old, weak, sick, and disabled" was sent back to Peking, and this time the list included both Mo-cun's and my names. I hadn't gotten to the point where I didn't want to return to Peking, but I had been hoping to return with all my companions. But then if there was a second group, it stood to reason that there would be a third, and a fourth...It looked like everyone in the cadre school would be returning to Peking in dribs and drabs, and I must admit that we were secretly pleased to be among the earlier ones to return. And our companions were so happy for us that they even hosted some farewell dinners. Since the stove in our dormitory had not yet been taken down, it was used to prepare glutinous-rice dumplings for our farewell dinners, as well as some meat-and-vegetable-filled won-tons, the vegetables for which we picked wild. All these people were also away from their homes, but their mood was much more generous than mine had been when seeing off the other group a year earlier. Looking into the faces of the "old, weak, sick, and disabled" whose names had not appeared on the current namelist filled me with a sense of guilt, but neither the guilt nor the gratitude I felt could suppress the selfish joy that filled my heart. I now understood something more clearly than ever: after undergoing more than ten years of reform, plus two years at the cadre school, not only had I not reached the plateau of progressive thinking that everyone sought, I was nearly as selfish now as I had been in the beginning. I was still the same old me.

It has now been eight years since I returned to Peking. So many little incidents are as fresh in my mind as if they had happened only yesterday, and since that period of my life has proved to be an invaluable experience, I have written these six chapters.

Translator's Afterword

ANYONE FAMILIAR WITH the works of Qian Zhongshu, particularly his novel *Fortress Besieged (Weicheng)*, knows that his words are not always to be taken at face value. So when we read in his Foreword (小引) to his wife's long reminiscence of their lives during the Cultural Revolution that the work after which it is patterned—Shen Fu's *Six Chapters of a Floating Life*[1]—is "a book I never did like," we must assume that the opposite may actually be closer to the truth. In many ways this account belongs as much to Qian as to Yang—which is not meant to detract from the author's virtuoso performance, but to point out the influence Qian and his wife have had on each other.

Yang Jiang's *Six Chapters from My Life "Downunder"* is a work of remarkable sophistication which, in its subtle, almost allegorical style, stands as powerful testimony to the insanity of the Cultural Revolution. Read carefully, it takes on added significance with implications for the entire revolutionary process. The author has chosen to describe life in a cadre school by recounting relatively insignificant

---

[1] 浮生六記, an autobiographical work by Shen Fu 沈復, recording his wedded bliss and subsequent trials and sorrows, first published in 1877; translated into English by Lin Yutang and included in *The Wisdom of China and India*. New York: Random House, 1942.

and commonplace events. Unlike the "wounded" (shanghen) literature of the post-1977 years, the Gang of Four is never mentioned in "Downunder." Jiang Qing is alluded to, but only obliquely when the author refers to a nearby locale called Tiger Mountain, the home of a vicious dog—calling to mind one of Jiang Qing's model operas, *Taking Tiger Mountain By Strategy*. Lin Biao is referred to by name when his death is mentioned, virtually without comment (unless the use of the slangy phrase 格兒庇着凉 —"kick the bucket"—can be considered a comment). With the leading culprits of China's "holocaust" thus removed, one could hardly be faulted for looking at the system and at the whole of recent Chinese history for the basic causes of the Cultural Revolution.

To say that Yang Jiang's writing style is low-key and subtle is in itself an understatement. To say that she skirts the major issues or important concerns of the time is to misread the piece entirely. Granted, most of what she has written is extremely personal and, seemingly, of a commonplace nature. In the long run, that, plus the occasional but poignant and fitting authorial comment, is what lends the piece such power.

Yang and her husband fared far better than many of their peers; that fact alone probably went a long way in saving the piece from becoming another narrowly focused "j'accuse." Without relating any "horror stories," the author has given us here her keen observation of the more pervasive effects of the Cultural Revolution's policies.

She makes the reader share in the overall sense of disappointment, frustration and skepticism directed at those people—or the system—responsible for what was visited upon her family and her fellow victims. Several themes emerge from her quiet, matter-of-fact narrative. One is the mutual distrust and general incompatibility between China's urban intellectuals (the "stinking old ninths") and the peasants who were their "masters;" this, of course, tends to invalidate the basic principle behind the *xiafang* movement. Another recurrent theme is waste—particularly the waste of human talent. The author frequently alludes to this by describing the useless or counterproductive activities required of young and old alike, but nowhere does the waste of human resources come through as clearly and alarmingly as in the succinctly told sequence involving the death of her son-in-law, Deyi.

There are other important themes in *"Downunder,"* such as the backwardness of the Chinese countryside, the nature of the "campaigns," and the demeanor of the people involved in them. This last theme is given particular emphasis in Qian's "Foreword." Probably the most touching theme of all, which becomes clearer with each reading, is the devotion between husband and wife, which, more than anything else, kept them going throughout their ordeal. Yang Jiang and Qian Zhongshu were lucky—they got to see each other on a more or less regular basis—but we can assume that the survival of vast numbers of couples (even when separated for years and by great distances) was a result of their mutual love and concern. So *"Downunder"* is also a love story, which, while describing a society in one of its darkest historical moments, reaffirms the endurance of humanity.

Six Chapters from My Life "Downunder" 幹校六記 by Yang Jiang was first published in issue 103 (April 1981) of

Editions of *Six Chapters from My Life "Downunder"*

(*Above left*) *Wide Angle Magazine*
(*Above right*) Wide Angle Publisher
(*Left*) Joint Publishing Company

the Hong Kong magazine *Wide Angle* 廣角鏡. In the following month it appeared in book form. Approximately a dozen printing errors were noted by the author in this edition. The Taiwan *United Daily News* (聯合報) subsequently reprinted the entire work, including Qian Zhongshu's "Foreword" and a short analysis by Ye Hongsheng 葉洪生, from July 21 to July 23, 1981; a few more errors crept into the text at this point. The definitive edition, now available in book form, was printed by the Joint Publishing Company 三聯書店 in the PRC and distributed by Xin Hua Book Store in July, 1981. In this edition, the author acknowledges the assistance of Hou Minze 侯敏澤, which probably constitutes an imprimatur for this sensitive work. (Hou subsequently published an article on the work, entitled "「幹校六記」讀後" in the September 1981 issue of 「讀書」).

Although the translation of *"Downunder"* began as a one-man project, it soon evolved into a cooperative venture that involved the efforts of the translator and two superb editors—Stephen Soong and George Kao of *Renditions.* Not only did Mr. Soong and Mr. Kao keep the translator's attention focused on Yang Jiang's low-key style, supply him with answers to elusive allusions and puns, and correct all his errors, but they are mainly responsible for the choice of title and chapter headings. It was felt that a literal translation of the title—something on the order of *Six Chapters of a Cadre School*—would mean little to many Western readers; *"Downunder"* is, of course, a reference to the "down to the countryside" 下放 movement, which led to the establishment of the May Seventh Cadre schools. The chapter headings, for which Mr. Kao can take credit, capture both the form and the rhythm of the original, four-character headings.

In order to make some of the material (specialized terminology, puns, allusions, etc.) more accessible to the reader, a few brief explanatory notes have been supplied in the text. More comprehensive notes have been included in the Background Notes, which follow, as an attempt to expand the base for understanding Yang's remarkable work without intruding upon the reader's right to personally experience and appreciate the sophistication and subtle force of the original.

The calligraphy on the covers of both editions of the original book is the work of Qian Zhongshu.

Background Notes

Chapter 1, P.5 Line 1

At the time when the author and her husband were sent down to the cadre school in 1969 and 1970, the Chinese Academy of Social Sciences was still called the Philosophy and Social Sciences Study Division of the Chinese Academy of Sciences (formerly Academia Sinica). It was not until the fall of the Gang of Four that the Study Division regained its normal research role and in 1978 was reorganized and renamed the Chinese Academy of Social Sciences, formally separated from the Chinese Academy of Sciences. It is divided into administrative, research and teaching branches and now consists of more than 3,000 staff members. Researchers like the author are equivalent to a full professor in rank and in salary. Senior Researchers like Qian Zhongshu hold a rank equivalent to that of the President of a University.

Chapter 1, P.6, Lines 9-10

"... we would soon be sent to a cadre school 'downunder'." The term "cadre school" is taken from a letter written by Mao Zedong to Lin Biao on May 7th, 1966, authorizing the PLA to "participate in the criticism of the capitalist class during the Cultural Revolution," embracing the schools, factories and countryside, since the PLA is itself a university. This was used as the basis for the military to take subsequent control of various organizations, institutes and schools. A cadre school, therefore, is not a school in the real sense of the term but a center of reeducation-through-labor for those who were suspended from their work. The first one was established when the Workers and PLA Propaganda Teams occupied and took over Qinghua (Tsinghua) University in 1968. During the early period of the Cultural Revolution, 1966-1971, all intellectuals were transferred down to the countryside, the research institutes were closed down and the universities suspended teaching, in order to construct their own cadre schools and undergo reeducation-through-labor. The intellectuals were labelled "stinking old ninths" (臭老九), derived from the classification of people into eight classes during the Yuan dynasty. Senior Researchers like Yu Pingbo, who is the pioneer and founder of the new school of *Dream of the Red Chamber* studies and a foremost authority on *ci* (lyrics), and Qian Zhongshu, a walking encyclopaedia of Chinese studies, were all required to do manual labor.

Chapter 1, P.6, Line 10

"downunder." As explained before, "downunder" is a free though accurate rendition of the term *xiafang* 下放 . The *xiafang* movement of 1956-57 was conceived to "transfer downward" the cadres from the cities to live together with factory workers and peasants. It was designed to create a deeper sense of mutual understanding between the ruling class and the ruled and to combat the growing sense of bureaucratism among the cadres.

Chapter 1, P.16, Line 12

"May Sixteenth" Elements. The May Sixteenth Army Corps was a group of ultra-leftist Red Guards formed on May 16th, 1967 and supported by Jiang Qing behind the scenes. Their chief targets were Zhou Enlai and his colleagues. It was outlawed in March 1968, and a liquidation process followed.

Chapter 2, P.23, Line 12

"didn't seem quite right, ideology-wise." The skit was found to be ideologically incorrect after the performance, partly owing to the absence of a central heroic figure, which could be considered contrary to Jiang Qing's demand for positive proletarian figures in all literary and dramatic works. More important still, the Volga Boatman were slave laborers in Tsarist Russia liberated by the October Revolution. The comparison would surely reflect on the prevalent situation in the PRC.

Chapter 2, P.24, Lines 13-14

"So we added a small vial of patent medicine to each bucketful [of water]." The original, *shayaoshui* 痧藥水 , is a popular patent medicine in liquid form, in use for more than half a century, which is supposed to possess curative powers for cholera, sunstroke, etc. To use it as a water purifier or disinfectant has more psychological than clinical value.

Chapter 2, P.30, Lines 13-15

"Constantly stooping over" and "turning the pulley". The originals are *dungong* 蹲功 and *zhuangong* 轉功 in quotation marks. They are derived from the word *gongfu* (Kung Fu) 功夫 , implying that long practice has made experts of the practitioners. The word *gong* is also applied to young apprentices of Peking Opera troupes who have to learn the basic skills of their trade in their early childhood.

Chapter 2, P.31, Line 15

"Cow sheds." The word cow (*niu*) 牛 stands for *niuguei sheshen* 牛鬼蛇神 (cow demons and snake spirits), which first appeared in a poem by Li He (Li Ho) and the *New Tang History*, and was again used in the *Dream of the Red Chamber*, which Mao loved to read; he used the term to label all reactionaries and bad elements, including his former close colleagues such as Liu Shaoqi. "Cow sheds" initially were temporary quarters used to detain intellectuals in the institutes and universities during the Cultural Revolution. Eventually, *xia niupeng* 下牛棚 came to mean downward transfer to cadre schools.

Chapter 3, P.33, Lines 2-4

"From each according to his ability, to each according to his needs" is the Marxist ideal for distribution in a socialist state; it was propounded in Marx's "Critique of the Gotha Program."

Chapter 3, P.47, Lines 27-28

"An earthen mound that looked like a huge steamed bun." The mound likened to an earthen steamed bun is derived from a couplet of a poem by the Song poet Fan Chengda (1126-1193).

Chapter 4, P.62, Line 4

"**the three-antis movement.**" Between 1952-53, a "three-antis" movement was launched to oppose corruption, waste and bureaucracy that existed among the cadres. It evolved into the "five-antis" movement aimed at the capitalistic and middle-class owners of private enterprises and industries, which were eventually nationalized.

Chapter 4, P.63, Lines 1-2

"**never sleep under a mulberry tree for three consecutive nights.**" One of the most famous anecdotes in the Buddhist sutras: the Buddha is not supposed to sleep under a mulberry tree for three consecutive nights for fear of becoming attached to that particular tree. It is a form of asceticism, the elimination of the seven emotions and six desires, being a preliminary requirement to holiness. In a cadre school, the temporary attachment to a little puppie would cause nothing but emotional involvement, which is highly undesirable.

Chapter 5, P.70, Lines 17-18

"**and weighted them down so heavily that it was as though eunuchs were vying to relieve me of my boots.**" The original *jyaulishi* 膠力士 , literally "gluey person of great physical strength," is a homonym in the Shanghai dialect of Gao Lishi 高力士 , a favorite eunuch of the Tang emperor, Ming Huang. Here the author feels that her rainboots are so glued to the sticky mud that they are forcibly being taken off by someone like Gao Lishi, who in the legendary anecdote, took off the boots of the great poet Li Bai after the latter had completed three lyrics for the favorite imperial concubine of Ming Huang and got himself drunk.

Chapter 5, P.71, Line 10

"**it [the ridge] crumbled as soon as it was touched.**" The original (*su-ti*) 酥隄 , a soaked and soft ridge, is a homonym of 蘇隄 . While the former refers to the ridge made of mud, which is completely softened by rain and crumbles under the impact of footsteps, the latter refers to 蘇公隄 , the famous Sugong Ridge of West Lake, built by the great Song poet Su Dongpo when he was the magistrate of Hangzhou.

Chapter 5, P.81, Lines 3-4

"study sessions." The original, *xuexi* 學習 (to study), is one of the most pervasive phenomena in the PRC. To study or learn the directives, documents, and guidelines, etc. issued by the Party, and be familiar with the essays, letters, and works of the current Party leaders, plays a most important role in the life of the people. It may be carried out privately or collectively, but inevitably culminates in public-discussion sessions in the unit to which one belongs.

Chapter 6, P.88, Line 26

"freedom is the appreciation of necessity." This is a translation of Engels' *Anti-Dühring* I, xi: "Für ihn [Hegel] ist die Freiheit die Einsicht in die Notwendigheit". In other words, freedom is not dictated by one's will but by circumstances.

Chapter 6, P.89, Lines 2-3

"decipher some of the hard-to-read Chinese characters." Qian was being highly esteemed by the local post office for the help rendered in deciphering some of the hard-to-read characters, mostly because they were written by poorly educated people incorrectly in simplified form. He was rewarded with glasses of tea. Of course, no one there had the slightest inkling that Qian was one of China's foremost textual critics. He studied paleography in Oxford and went to the Bodleian Library to examine the ancient manuscripts written on sheep skins. He has often been consulted as the final authority on textual problems and the correct reading of certain characters given in various editions. To think that he is now revered and utilized by a tiny post office, which cannot be found on the map, is more than a waste of talent and wealth of knowledge. It is one of the most poignant ironies in the work.

Chapter 6, P.93, Line 18

"through the fire and crucible of reform." The original *jiuzheng jiubei*, 九蒸九焙 , may be literally translated as: "steamed nine times and baked nine times", an idiom of the Shanghai dialect. It describes the elaborate process of preparing Chinese medicine by steaming a mixture of Chinese herbs in liquid form and baking it, finally reducing it to either jelly or pills.

"a barefoot doctor." The establishment of the practice of "barefoot doctors" began in 1964 and was extremely prevalent during the latter part of the Cultural Revolution. Whereas patients formerly visited the doctors in clinics and hospitals, the process was reversed so that the doctors were required to go to the factories and countryside to visit the patients — in other words, to serve the people. Many of the teaching staff of various medical colleges and schools were transferred "downunder" to cadre schools in order to be near the peasants, while others were deprived of teaching duties and required to do manual labor. Furthermore, the regular training period of a medical student, lasting six to seven years, was considered much too long and wasteful. The pre-medical courses and theoretical teaching, therefore, were suspended so that a greater number of students could be turned out within a short period of time by learning the treatment of the most common forms of illness with the aid of a rudimentary knowledge of acupuncture. These "instant" doctors formed the backbone of the corps of "the barefoot doctors" that covered the nation. However, the number of doctors was far from being adequate to meet the needs of nearly a billion people. So in the author's cadre school, there was only an unqualified nurse who gave Qian the first intravenous injection of her life and by sheer luck saved Qian from serious illness.

About the Translator

HOWARD GOLDBLATT has been responsible for introducing several modern and contemporary Chinese writers to English-speaking audiences: his biography of the Northeastern Chinese novelist Xiao Hong (Hsiao Hung, 1911-1942) and his translations of three of her novels—*The Field of Life and Death* (1979), *Tales of Hulan River* (1979), and *The Misadventures of Ma Bo-le* (to be published in 1984)—and a volume of her short stories (1983), have helped establish her as an international literary figure. He is also the co-translator of the celebrated *The Execution of Mayor Yin* by Chen Jo-hsi (1978) and the translator of *The Drowning of an Old Cat* by the Taiwanese writer Hwang Chun-ming (1980), as well as the author of many articles in Chinese and English on modern Chinese literature. He is an associate professor of Chinese literature at San Francisco State University.